Athletes, coaches, sport leaders and parents on *A Mind to Win* and the SportExcel System

Athlete's Perspective

"As a professional surfer you can lose your focus at a competition because of distractions from sponsors, spectators, weather, etc. Bob helped me to stay focused and aggressive on every wave."

— **ALANA BLANCHARD**, Professional Association of Surfing Professionals (ASP), Women's World Championship Tour, Hawaii

"Bob was the first mental coach that I worked with at the beginning of my career. His methods became some of the fundamentals that I used as part of my everyday routine. The knowledge that I have learned from him has helped me achieve my ultimate dream."

— **VINCENT HANCOCK,** Two-Time Olympic Gold Medalist, International Skeet, USA

"I set my sights on becoming a pro hockey player and Bob has helped me to find the Zone at every stage of my development."

— **NORM EZEKIEL**, Pro Hockey Player, Canada

"This is the revolutionary aspect of Bob's program. It helps you change your mind, and your physiology by using the Zone experience as the central focus of your everyday activities."

— **SARA GROSS**, Professional Ironman Triathlete (Podium, Brazil 2013) and Coach, Canada

"Working closely with Bob in the years leading into the Olympic Games was an incredible experience. I learned a lot about the power of the mind and the subconscious, and I gained a better appreciation for the work that needs to be done not only on the track, but off the track. My work with Bob provided tools to face any feat, small or large, with a clear mind and a confidence that allowed me to perform freely and in the moment. As an athlete there's nothing comparable to the feelings of performing in the moment, which made every session with Bob very rewarding."

— **JESSICA ZELINKA**, Canadian Champion and Record holder in Heptathlon, two-time Olympian, Canada

"Your incredible talent to share the Zone with me has allowed me to grow in ways I never imagined possible! Thank you for sharing this magic with me and making the world a better place...one Zone Feel at a time."

— **GABI VITERI**, Retired Professional Burton Snowboarder, USA

"The time you spent with me has been paying off. I thank you tremendously. This is a 90 percent mental and 10 percent physical game. I wish I knew you when I was a kick boxer in my younger days."

— **SCOTT HILL**, Former World Kickboxing Champion, Canada

Coach's Perspective

"Since working with Bob late last year, not only have we made an improvement to my mental game, but I also have a much better understanding of the Zone."

— **PAUL GIAMBRONE III**, 14-time World Champion and
Skeet Coach, USA

"Masterfully written!! It should be on the must read list of every serious competitor in any sport."

— **STEVE BROWN**, Sporting Clays Coach, USA

"Bob Palmer has worked with my elite athletes. Not only was there a remarkable transformation of the individual athletes, but also a strong team bonding. He will continue to be an integral part of our training program."

— **LES GREEVY**, U.S. Olympic (Clay Target)
Coach of the Year 2004, USA

Sport/Business Leader's Perspective

"As a High Performance Director of a National Sport Organization, like any elite athlete or businessman, I need to be in the Zone; I need to be at my best. Bob's program helped me in all aspects of my work and my game and I use his system on a daily basis."

— **BOB JONCAS**, High Performance Director, Snowboard Canada

"As a retired US Navy SEAL and athlete, who has been able to get to the highest levels that my physical ability could take me in many sports, I will tell you that what Bob has learned and is teaching in this book is what you have been seeking. Read it, learn it, practice it, become the Zone! IT'S A LOT OF FUN!!"

— **DR. JOE LACAZE**, Retired US Navy Seal,
Doctor of Chiropractic, USA

"I'd finally found exactly what I was looking for — a simple, effective and easy to use system for enhancing performance and productivity, delivered with passion and expertise. I've now integrated the system in my own strategies and work and get value from it every day. I highly recommend you check out Bob's approach to high performance because I know it works."

— **PETER BAEKLUND**, Founder & Head Coach,
Peter Baeklund Resourceful Leadership, Denmark

"Bob gives athletes an unfair advantage!"

— **RON HANSELL**, CEO and Executive Athlete, Canada

"With boring regularity I get into the Zone and win with Bob's system. We only lost one curling match in the last month and I play on five teams in five different leagues."

— **LES FRASER,** Consultant and Executive Athlete, Canada

Parent's Perspective

"MacKenzie is a completely different player since working with Bob. In the last tournament she scored half of the team's 15 goals. She has more confidence and fun and has developed a scoring touch around the net."

— **Anita Klein**, Mother of a 14-year old hockey player, Canada

"My son worked as hard as he could on the field but always seemed to come up short. Bob helped him (and us) to gain the pizzazz that got the coaches noticing. And he has been improving and having more fun in every practice and game since the training. The lessons he learned from Bob will last him a lifetime."

— **CM**, Mother of a young football player, Canada

"My wife and I now have an active role that we never had before and it makes a considerable difference. Thanks for the work you have put into this program and we would recommend it to anyone wanting to advance, regardless of the endeavor."

— **GREG ELLIOTT**, Parent of a young athlete, USA

A Mind to Win

Kicking your game into overdrive

Bob Palmer

SportExcel Inc.

Copyright © 2014 SportExcel Inc.

All rights reserved.

No part of this book may be reproduced, distributed or scanned in any printed or electronic form without the permission of the publisher. Please do not participate in or encourage piracy of copyrighted materials in violation of the author's rights. Purchase only authorized editions.

ISBN: 978-0-9917618-5-2

Published by SportExcel Inc.

www.sportexcel.ca

bpalmer@sportexcel.ca

Disclaimer

The information contained in this book is made available by SportExcel Inc. It is to be used strictly for educational purposes only. SportExcel Inc. does not offer any psychological, professional, medical, financial, personal or legal advice and none of the information contained in this book should be confused as such advice. Results of using the System may vary from individual to individual.

For Caron and her inspiration and partnership in this project

Acknowledgments

Grateful acknowledgment is made to the following people for their contribution to the writing and creation of this book:

My blended family for their support throughout this project.

Robert VandenDool for creating the original artwork for the book cover, for providing creative collaboration on the cover design and for being a great guy.

Caron Palmer, for project management and cover design.

Dan Parle, Media Expert, for editing and professional advice.

Dr. John Grinder and Derek Balmer for their inspirational NLP concepts.

E. A Feliu, poet, artist and passionate athlete for his poetic contribution.

David Goodreau for allowing us to share his passion for snowboarding on the back cover of the book.

Adam Forbes for the use of his back-cover photograph.

Sensei Masaru Shintani and my other senseis and martial arts colleagues for inspiring me to dig deep and figure it out.

Contents – The SportExcel System

The Zone

The hardest part was not thinking.

Not what was before, not what was after.

The now. The moment. The action.

The body knows by feeling.

When electricity travels

through the filament, the bulb glows.

When the wire snaps, continuity stops.

Such is the power of overwhelming thought.

It must be like peeling an orange

without consulting the hands, eyes fixed

on a momentous cloud.

Seeing becomes a way of thinking.

Moment by moment, the body pulses

with the telegraphs of feeling.

— **E. A Feliu,** poet, artist and passionate athlete, lives in San Diego, CA. He has published a poetry collection, *Postcards from the Tattooed Man's Chest,* and is working on a second book - a collection of sports poems. He may be reached at eafeliu@yahoo.com

Foreword by Hannah Teter

After the 2006 Turin Olympics, where I won gold, the half pipe snowboarding event evolved into an exciting, very competitive and specialized sport. The IOC changed the structure of the half pipe so that it had much higher amplitude (but no softer a landing). Unfortunately, during one of my training sessions at the new height, I had a train wreck and partially dislocated my shoulder. This was mere months from the 2010 Olympics. So, with the new height, my injury and my self-imposed pressure to repeat in Vancouver, you can understand that my confidence might have been just a bit off.

In January 2010, about eight weeks out from the Vancouver Olympics, my coach went in search of a professional who would help me to get my Turin "golden touch" back. He stumbled upon Bob Palmer of SportExcel on his first surf of the Internet. He called Bob and tried to convince him that I only needed my confidence back. Bob told him that he didn't deliver psychology or confidence, but if I wanted the tools to win, he would help me get well, get in the Zone and get that podium finish I wanted.

So we began our preparation for the games, skeptically I must add, but in ten or so sessions he introduced me to his system and a whole new world of high performance. First he helped me forget that I had ever injured my shoulder. I could barely remember the accident and could feel no pain. It was amazing. Second, when I told him how sympathetic my teammates were and how on a daily basis they would ask about my shoulder, he laughed. "They aren't concerned about your shoulder," he said, "But they want *you* to be." I didn't believe they would ever do a thing like that, but in the next training session it became very obvious. Bob helped me understand the new reality of competition and how it was normal for my teammates to have only one goal and that was to beat me. After that my coach began to put up a protective shield around me during training.

Bob also taught me how to forget bad competitions, how to learn new tricks by modeling other Olympians like Shaun White, how to visualize the Vancouver half pipe so it felt like I'd been there many times before, how to remove the fear of crashing again and how to make spectators and opponents disappear so that it was just me on the half pipe (along with the smiling judges). One of the neatest things Bob taught me was called the A-BUTTON, a button I could mentally push to get instantly wired with just the right amount of adrenaline before I drop into the pipe.

Well, the rest is history. I bounced back from my injury and in just a few weeks I re-qualified for the U.S. Olympic Team. And then, in Vancouver, under less than ideal conditions, I pulled off a silver medal. Considering what I had gone through, it was glorious. I was stoked.

I worked with Bob in person, and he is still my high performance strategist, but his book gives all athletes the same great system I learned. Every pro or aspiring athlete can benefit from learning it — for sport, work, school and life.

— Hannah Teter, Pro-snowboarder and three-time Olympian;
Olympic Gold and Silver medalist and X Games medalist

Why You Need This Book — For
Ongoing Brilliance

"There is always one moment in childhood
when the door opens and lets the future in."

— **Graham Greene,** *Star Writer*

Brilliant images of successful pro and Olympian athletes fill the media. The magic of their play opens up a world of possibilities, sparks our dreams and ignites our passion. As kids, we subconsciously step into their shoes on a playground that looks convincingly like the big stadium, arena or pool. We become these great athletes and we acquire exceptional joy in this fantasy. Our play has newfound skill and the cup gets hoisted, the medals get won, and the dramatic "believable" experience is duplicated over and over, victory after victory.

It feels so wonderful and the game feels so easy in this imaginary world. Unfortunately that good feeling becomes tainted and disappears for most of us the longer we play our sport, mostly from frustrating and discouraging experiences. But it needn't. And that is why I have written this book for you — athlete, coach, CEO or trainer — to help you to overcome those kinds of experiences and rekindle the passion of your game.

This book is designed to give you a system that will reconnect you to your dreams so that you can rediscover the fun of playing to win, just like you did as a child, and just as effortlessly.

The athletes I work with intuitively know the game is easy. They know because they've experienced individual moments of brilliance — like magic, without any conscious attempt to be confident or positive or breathe. In that instant their game becomes magically, wonderfully and powerfully fun, with an effortless, timeless and non-thinking quality to it.

You may be one of the fortunate few to have experienced this. What happens to us in these moments of brilliance? Is it indeed magical or can we take steps to make it happen every time, on demand? In his book, *The Talent Code*, Daniel Coyne talks about special coaches who are *Igniters* of their students, who then achieve extraordinary results — sustained brilliance. Since many of you lack that kind of coach, you will need to do it for yourself. YOU will have to be the *self-igniter* of your own brilliance.

A Mind To Win takes a six-step approach to helping you to ignite your game *all by yourself* — a step-by-step, no emotions, systems-based approach to the mental game — so that your best, most skillful "moment of brilliance" can be repeated, over and over and over, time and again, on demand. In this book you learn to flip a high performance switch, which will allow you to take your moments of brilliance to your entire game, season and career. You get to ignite your strategic, precise, empowered, all-action and skillful game. And you have the opportunity to have fun, take strategic leadership of your team, and win too.

On this journey you'll learn the tools to fix nervousness and intimidation; to resolve mental lapses and slumps with no need to talk about them or even understand what is causing them; to increase your power, speed, smarts, strength and skill by modeling pros and Olympians; and to lead your team or fellow athletes with passion, motivation and drive. This is all part of the system that you will learn in this book.

A Mind to Win is a system for winning, and athletes love it, as it has helped many win at the amateur, Olympic and professional levels — Olympic gold medals included! And they keep on winning, with additional championships in state high-school, pole vaulting, Olympic-level hurdles and amateur golf as I write this.

This book (and the system therein) opens the door to a revolution that is occurring in sport, as it puts you in charge, with no talk and no need to delve into, and (mis)understand, the past. Just turn the key, fire up your passion as you did when you were a child and create some magic. Learning to win is fun, as you will soon experience. All it takes is a system and, of course, your vivid dreams. Enjoy.

Bob Palmer

— **Bob Palmer, B.Ed., B.E.S., Barrie, Ontario, Canada**

1 Learning to Win

---

*The heights this book will take you, if you are willing
to stop thinking and just play.*

*"We are what we repeatedly do. Excellence then,
is not an act, but a habit."*

— Aristotle, Star Philosopher

Let's not mince words. The main goal of this book is to help you
to win in your game (and life), whether that means winning the
bragging rights at the club, winning an Olympic gold medal, winning a
professional contract, winning a spot on the high school team or, simply,
winning in the improvement game through on-going skill development.
And although winning is the ultimate goal, your enjoyment of sport is what
is going to drive you to that perfect victory. The combined forces of
winning and enjoyment are inseparable. They affect all aspects of your
game, from the team you strive to play for to the financial impact of turning
pro, from the type of high-end equipment you buy to your commitment to
practice, compete and put in your time.

Whether you are a novice or a professional, this book will help you to create your own definition of high performance in order to win. From the get-go, I'll make no promises that this book will help you to win a high school, club or world championship, but you will certainly learn a system and the tools that will help you to do so. And I challenge you to see if you can apply them as effectively and successfully as the many athletes I have worked with have done in numerous sports. Only you can dictate that, along with how you read and apply this book to help you to achieve your dreams.

The Starting Point

This book is the starting point where you will understand what you learned or didn't learn from all your competitive experience — from playing Little League baseball, football, hockey or other sports, to your latest attempts to win. High performance is the process of doing anything well. It is staying sharp, event after event, and understanding the nature of the distractions that conspire to pull you out of that focus. Whether you are a novice or a professional, feel free to dream and to strive for your dreams as you read and apply the strategies in this book. I challenge you to be unrealistic and to go for it.

Creation of a System

There was once a high performance expert who, at age ten, knew there was more. Then, his target was a hockey net, and he played from sunup to sundown — full out — maniacally. It was wondrous. The outside world was nonexistent. Score seemed of no consequence but it meant everything to win the imagined cup. He enjoyed the euphoria, but never had a word for it.

But sadly, the organized version on an official ice rink threw this young expert into disarray. His game was lackluster and he could blame it on no one. Coaches, referees and opponents — who knew? But he knew the difference between his frustrating performances and his good ones, and he reveled in the rare moments — those moments of brilliance that stood out like a gold nugget in a pan of sand.

A fireball of energy might best have described him during those brief moments. He was skillful and unstoppable and, on a couple of occasions, there were unexpected moments where, at the end of the game, the opposing coach would pop into his team's dressing room to praise his play. Ah, but his own coach would be rolling his eyes and sighing, as that kind of play was extremely rare for this budding high performance expert.

How had this young athlete achieved these moments of brilliance and incredible skill, endurance and awareness, when, as far as he knew then, he had done nothing different? Had he read a book on psychology? No. Had his coach suddenly turned into a grand motivator? No. Had the other team beaten up his smaller teammate and got him ripping mad? Well, yes, on one occasion. Even then the question of "how" left an indelible imprint on his brain — a mystery unsolved, a few more nuggets of gold surrounded by too much sand. But it was enough to start him on his quest for the mother lode.

That young man kept pursuing that dream, even at the age thirty-five — in karate. Surely, it was insight gained from maturity. He was older, with an education, life experience and he found himself surrounded by fabulous mentors, role models and coaches. But there he was again, the skillful athlete with no pizzazz. Something big was dragging him down, distracting him. He was being reacquainted with the "dragons" of his childhood — surely what had hampered his success as a young hockey player. He could have gone the psychology route and been assessed and talked at for hours at length. But he felt so messed up that he would have been in therapy for the rest of his life. There were tournaments around the corner and he needed a fix now.

On the verge of quitting, he began to unravel the mystery of high performance through a mix of experience, education and luck, lots of luck. Slowly, but surely, this former perennial loser found himself using strategies that were working and helping him to win. He was succeeding in caging and/or training the dragons and, in doing so, developed a system that helped him to win a national championship in his karate organization.

A Repeatable System

That athlete was, of course, me. And the discovery that a simple, repeatable system could be so powerful and easy to implement was very exciting. Since that time, I have fine-tuned and taught my system to amateur, Olympic and professional athletes around the world, from 11-year-old aspiring hockey players to professional ones, mature curlers to professional Ironman triathletes. And now, I'm teaching it to you.

A Mind to Win is designed to help you to apply the SportExcel System at any ability or level. As a beginning athlete, almost everything in this book will be new and exciting so that you can improve at a very rapid rate. As an advanced athlete and/or coach, you can fill in your performance gaps by learning new tools and by understanding the tools that you are already using so that you use them much more effectively.

Six Steps to Winning

The SportExcel System is delivered in six steps, that, when combined with good, solid, sports skills, forms the foundation for unbeatable high performance. And the system can be applied to everything you do — sport, school, work and pleasure.

Step 1

Step 1 of the SportExcel System is the equivalent to the X Factor of television notoriety. I call it the Zone, the wonderful holy grail of sport (and life). Pick up any athlete's autobiography and you'll find a description of awesome feats of strength, playing with injury, uncanny anticipation, slowing down time, achieving perfect consistency game after game, snatching victory in the face of overwhelming odds and playing without thinking. The ZONE is our starting point, unlike other approaches to the mental game where the Zone is the endpoint. Making it the starting point, as you will see, makes the game a lot easier.

Step 2

Step 2 of the SportExcel System is the outcome, also known as the prize, goal, win, etc. It represents where you want to go and is the means by which you'll know if you are making progress in your game. An outcome can be any number of things, from the ideal equipment you want, to your career expectations.

Unlike other approaches where you write down your goals and read them every day, Step 2 of the SportExcel System is more about making your goals feel doable by creating passion and excitement for them, as well as adding a touch or two of adrenaline. My findings over a decade of working with athletes show that athletes can quickly transform their dreams into powerful, well-adrenalized parts of THEIR LIFE, so that they become déjà vu-like experiences. The goals simply feel DOABLE — and DONE — which makes them your OUTCOME!

Step 3

Step 3 of the SportExcel System is your guidance or feedback system, and since it is similar in nature to how a Global Positioning System (GPS) in your car keeps you on track as you move to your destination, we'll call this step GPS. It is all the elements of your game that you are aware of — win, lose or draw — and how you handle those elements.

You'll often hear, "You'll learn more from your mistakes and losses than from your wins." Maybe; *but it's unlikely*. That will only happen if you learn the tools to help you to do that. You'll also be told to use "process" (the steps to performing a skill) rather than focus on the "outcome" (of winning), because thinking about outcome will only get you distracted or panicky or discouraged or, even, overly optimistic. Wrong. Forget it all. Step 3 of the SportExcel System will teach you how to enjoy any and all guidance so that you can get to your destination. And it is GPS — the good, bad and ugly scores, moods, teammates and weather — that will teach you so much. Most importantly, you'll understand the role of score in your game. I mean, let's be realistic. As I said at the outset, score is the chief reason why are you competing in your game in the first place.

Step 4

Step 4 of the SportExcel System represents the strategies — the bulk of this book — that will help you to get back on track when distractions derail you. After so many years of being told to be confident (what is confidence?) and being told to park my bad memories (my parking lot became a piled up junk heap), I had to find another way.

Step 4 of the SportExcel System is the set of tools that will help you to forget mistakes, remove distractions, deal with difficult people and take leadership of your team, etc. — all at the subconscious level without having to think. When you have a problem, such as an overly critical coach who is pulling you out of the Zone with his negativity, you'll learn to fix that problem and move on so that you can play, not think!

Step 5

Step 5 of the SportExcel System pulls it all together. It allows the inner workings of your mind to stay inner and working, without your external interference — often called thinking. Your subconscious mind is very capable, and, *once trained*, can play exceptionally well. Your subconscious mind, *once trained*, can deal with any distraction. And, your subconscious mind, *once trained*, can fit your game/sport/passion/job into your life. Quite often I work with athletes whose problems in their game are unrelated to skill, equipment or ability to get in the Zone. It's work, school and other personal distractions that pop into their heads at the wrong time. Step 5 will highlight the inner workings of your internal, subconscious dynamics so that you learn how to create great ATTITUDE.

Step 6

Step 6 of the SportExcel System is all about you, as it is YOU who has to stick to the program. I've been there, so have hundreds of my very successful and happy athletes. Now it's your turn.

Taking Action

So let's get started, as this book is more than just a good read. It is a specially designed high-performance system that will take very little effort but lots of focused, consistent work. It will make all aspects of your game come to life — your short-term and long-term goals, your competition skills, your routines and the specific skills of your training. This system to achieving a consistent high performance is akin to a map leading to the mother lode that prospectors dream about. As a high-performing athlete, you can stop dreaming and start learning the skills required to find your sport mother lode and win.

The SportExcel System is loaded with tools that, with consistent work, will assist you for the rest of your competitive career and your life. Keep the book handy, because it is a resource. When you reach an impasse in your game or simply need a refresher, you can refer to the appropriate chapter and review the tools. It is designed to be read — and reread.

So be prepared to ratchet up your game a notch or 20.

High performance: Power, focus, strength, agility, flexibility and acute perception.

High performance: Time slows; thoughts disappear; anticipation is incredible.

Winning by achieving and maintaining this kind of high performance is the mission of this book — your mission. Get ready, as the key to igniting your Zone awaits you in the next chapter. So is all the new fun you'll begin having in your game.

Step 1

Igniting Your Zone

Life in the Fun Lane

"A mind that is stretched to a new idea
never returns to its original dimensions."
— Anonymous, Star Genius

STEP 1 – THE ZONE

Ignite The Zone → Excel

2 The Zone

Is it Real or Mythical?

"The less effort, the faster and more powerful you will be."
— ***Bruce Lee, Star Actor and Martial Artist***

Immediately after my workshops, participants rush to test out their newfound tools. They are skeptics wishing to test and verify. And they usually surprise themselves. Awareness is greater. Vision is sharper. Their equipment seems light and an extension of their arms. Net openings seem huge. Mistakes seem irrelevant — just a means to readjust. Much has changed for these athletes and they are now in control of their game — and smiling. They have found the first most important component of the system, the Zone.

So what is the Zone? Is it real or mythical? A perfect definition of the Zone is impossible, as every athlete who has ventured into that realm has his or her own. Based on findings from many client responses, a definition would be:

> *The Zone is a sense where sport is fun and easy, no matter what the conditions, and the game unfolds effortlessly*
> *WITH NO THINKING.*
> *More importantly, the Zone generates essential, ongoing agility, speed, decisiveness, strength, endurance and skillfulness.*

As for whether or not it is real, I'll leave that up to you to decide as you read this book in your quest to achieve it.

No Secret

Achieving the Zone is less a "secret" that someone has been hiding from you all these years and more a misunderstanding by well-meaning and well-educated people. They got sidetracked by their own inability to achieve it or by their misplaced observations regarding the successful athletes who have found the Zone. I've read articles that describe the Zone as a potential detriment to success if you try too hard to achieve it before properly developing your skills. I can only shake my head at such misleading comments.

Yet it is easy to understand how we have been misled, as the Zone often appears in random bursts of excellence that come out of nowhere, at bizarre moments and exits with no clues as to how to repeat it. Even the best athletes, who usually live in the Zone, are unsure of what it is exactly, as they developed it at a very early age (with no deliberate action or deep thinking). As a result, their sage advice to the rest of us can get lost in translation.

The Zone gives an incredible sense of awareness — sight, sound and feel. As an athlete, you have the perception that other people are slow. You seem to know what others are going to do next. You feel incredibly strong with incredible endurance. Quite simply, the Zone is a pleasant and satisfying state of euphoria where the game unfolds by itself and it seems all too easy.

The Zone is a Skill

No athletic skill needs to be attached to the Zone because the Zone is a skill in itself. Beginners can feel absolutely euphoric and still make mistake after mistake in the learning process. In so doing, however, they will learn very quickly with no frustration or discouragement. And with proper coaching, they can move up through the ranks, exercising and practicing both their athletic skill and their Zone skill.

So, the Zone is a skill that is a pleasant and satisfying euphoria within the context of a skillful game. And as soon as you add that last part — the pressure of competition, dreams of being a collegiate star, a pro, an Olympian or a measurement of yourself against your peers — the achievement and maintenance of the Zone becomes a lot more challenging, interesting and fun.

Four Levels of the Zone Skill

I've come up with four arbitrary levels of the Zone Skill. The first level is simply a learning stage of fun and play where you have no expectations to win and the challenge is to score. The second level is where you put yourself in the position of competing against your peers.

The third level is where you put yourself in a position of expecting to beat your peers. And the last level is where you KNOW the game is yours — opponents, score, weather, equipment quality and losing have no say in the matter — and it is all just fun and play.

Skill Level One

About five years ago, I was listening to a radio interview with Mickey Rooney. He was asked what he thought was the key to his success as an actor. Rooney responded with a question of his own to the interviewer: "When did you stop being creative?" he asked. There was some stammering by the interviewer and clear irritation in his voice. "I don't think I ever lost it," he huffed.

The point Rooney was trying to make was that the key to his success was his ability to play, even under the glare of cameras, retake after retake, and stay creative. Happy, creative children, own the Zone. They play, in the sandbox and with dress-up, totally absorbed in their activity. Even with parents watching, their focus is totally fixated on play.

The following are examples of a Level One Zone: Toddlers in a dance recital who are oblivious to the audience; young athletes who pick up the game for the first time and are in total awe of the physicality of it; adult golfers on the practice range where there is no pressure and whiffing a ball has no impact on their "perfect" game.

In his book, I Call The Shots, golfer Johnny Miller describes his youthful prowess where he was a putting phenomenon. He notes that kids live in another world. They rely on faith, optimism and hope — and it works. But he also notes that the Zone at Stage One is short lived. We lose

the Zone (or stop practicing it) via the pressures of life's experiences —
parents, coaches or our own expectations. We learn to feel bad about being
watched (put on the spot), about losing (only stupid people lose), about
being put down (others are so much better than us). This, of course, sets
the stage for the Level Two Zone Skill.

Skill Level Two

Many athletes have experienced the Level Two Zone Skill. It is the
kind of Zone that occurs serendipitously when you are under pressure,
deadline or attack. It often happens at the height of crisis situations when
you are being watched, are self-conscious or are afraid of making mistakes.
You feel sick and your brow, hands and underarms are dripping with sweat.

And then it happens — whether it is the tone of the coach's voice, a
gut reaction to a buddy having a complete meltdown or a flush of
adrenaline at being embarrassed — you get a shot of adrenaline and enter
an altered state where you play better than ever. You feel like you can
walk on water. But darn, it is fleeting and nearly impossible to get back to
it when you lose it. And as hard as you work to get all the conditions that
you think evoked it, the Zone remains elusive. Sadly, not many people get
beyond this stage.

Skill Level Three

The next level is simply more of Level Two, a whole lot more. Those
who get to Level Three — because of physical ability, lots and lots of
success, great role models, ability to shut themselves off from the world to
practice and perfect their technique, a powerful commitment, delight in
showing off, or even good genes — find themselves in the Zone on a

regular basis. Since it feels euphoric and is very addicting, the athletes soon learn how to live in, and know the FEEL of it. Usually, they can get the FEEL of the Zone before they start their game.

Most professional athletes are at a Level Three Zone. But it, too, is not as stable as they would like it to be. Think of the number of really skillful athletes who only survive a year in the big leagues. Success at Level Three can be hard to maintain because it is based on the repetition of success. At this level, there is little knowledge of how they got into the Zone. Put any Level Three player on a losing team, with a negative coach, negative teammates, a depressed spouse, an attention deficit and hyperactive disordered child (ADHD) or a chronic injury — and they too will falter.

Skill Level Four

The last and highest level of the Zone is different. It's not just a lot more of Level Three. In this case, the athletes have had their share of success as they came through Level Three, but through failure, defeat, more defeat, other adversity, luck or modeling others — they have somehow learned the tools to overcome and forget all the bad stuff. Their heads are only filled with good thoughts and fabulous outcomes.

Level Four athletes build character and retain that character. They sometimes develop late, overcome injuries, rise above difficult childhoods, create winning teams out of losing ones, thrive in problem-solving situations, etc. They never give up. They experiment all the time and make up for any physical deficits with passion, hard work and flexibility. When they get injured they figure out what it takes to come back. When they lose, they figure out what to do so it will never happen again. When they fall apart in a critical play-off, they train even harder for the next competition. When they feel intimidated by coaches or other athletes, they figure out how to overcome it.

One of my karate instructors was my role model for this. He would come back from losing in a competition and learn the technique that had beaten him. He would practice that technique over and over until he knew it better than his opponent. Nobody ever beat him with the same technique twice.

An amazing thing happens to athletes at a Level Four Zone. They start to play and be creative. With that creativity, they design new sets of skills that set the standard and break records. If a Level One Zone teaches us that an athlete can play and be in the Zone without skills, a Level Four Zone teaches us that an athlete can be in the Zone with skill and the game becomes play. And when you play you stay creative. Mickey Rooney had it right. To maintain your creativity, you have to learn to play.

The Zone is Play

Play is serious business. The more seriously you strive to be playful and the more seriously you work at your game with a sense of joy and humor, the sooner your skills will allow you to pass from Level One play to Level Four play. In the next chapter I'll teach you a way to get the Zone from the get-go. It is called reverse engineering, where you'll capture the FEEL of success from past moments of brilliance and use it as a guide to extended periods of brilliance.

Get ready to play!

3 Reverse Engineering the Zone

How we can know before we play, that we will
perform well.

"Any training that does not include the emotions, mind and body,
is incomplete; knowledge fades without feeling."

— Anonymous, Star Genius

After a recent international event, I asked a new client what had happened during the games to keep him out of the medal round. He described all manner of distractions from equipment failures to a very new experience with a sizable and vocal crowd of spectators. "It affected everyone", he said. "Everyone?" I asked. "Well", he added, "except for the eventual winner. That athlete seemed unfazed by it all." I smiled, because I had trained the winning athlete.

It took one look at the video footage of the competition to see how clearly that athlete stood out from the field. Everything about him indicated the Zone. His posture was tall and erect and by sheer physical impact he seemed larger than his opponents. I explained this to my new client and he was intrigued, but skeptical. I smiled, as I knew that he was about to experience something he had already experienced many times previously — the Zone — only from here on in it would be on demand.

Being in the Zone is an incredible and on-going personal, exhilarating experience. Most elite athletes know the Zone. And I can assure you that you have experienced it as well, in a very clear and specific way. It was empowering to you in sport, at work or in school. To others you displayed an incredible sense of confidence (and sometimes "cockiness"); you, however, may have missed what they saw. So, in this step, you are going to:

1) Remember an experience that was successful (Zone-like),

2) Identify the feeling of the Zone (in a specific way with a specific signal), and,

3) Learn to repeat the Zone every time you play your game (by getting the signal).

1) Remembering Your Successes

We all have a wealth of great experiences in sport and/or in other areas of our lives. Thinking of these experiences as the Zone is unfamiliar territory — a few moments here, a few rounds or quarters there, perhaps an unexpected day of pure joy. I have yet to find anyone who is so perfectly awful that he or she consistently makes mistakes. You all have moments and you may need to search your mind to find them, but these are your moments of brilliance — they are your starting point. These experiences, believe it or not, are you in the Zone. The stronger your memory of these events — with sight, sound and feeling — the more powerful they will be in terms of helping you to identify your signal for the Zone.

2) Identifying Your Zone FEEL

Next we want to identify your Zone specifically by Zone FEEL — as it will give you a precise way of knowing when you are in it before you play your game. It is relatively easy to identify someone else's Zone and whether he or she is going to play well — there's a level of focus, calm attention and certainty. There's the solid posture. There's the soft gaze. It is also relatively easy for others to see it in you, too — but, unfortunately, there is no mirror you can hold up in front of yourself as you play your game. Nor can you have your coach perched on your shoulder to remind you. Nor can you guide yourself with self-talk. The first two are silly, the last requires thinking.

We need another way, one that is truly obvious to us — blatantly obvious. And we'll find it in your ability to feel an internal sensation, the kind of internal sensation you get when you swell up with pride after a wonderful accomplishment. Your body just feels good with tingles as your chest expands, your core warms, and your gut flutters with good butterflies. For those of you with limited memories of successful accomplishments, the sensation you are looking for (feeling for) may be similar to the warm feeling you get after you drink a hot cup of cocoa. We'll call this sensation Zone FEEL, and it needs to be as evident and as clear as a traffic signal that indicates the intersection is safe (or not), a camcorder recording light that indicates you are recording successfully (or not), and the sound of an egg timer that indicates the egg is perfectly cooked (or not). If you want a repeatable Zone, you require an identifiable signal, an internal sensation that is clearly unmistakable, just as in the three examples noted above.

Elite athletes develop this Zone FEEL "sweet-spot" over time through success, diligent work or sheer luck. Somehow the rest of us missed out, so we need to develop our own sweet spot now, by taking stock of our past successes and noticing what they tell us. That is where your moments of brilliance come in, however great or insignificant they may have appeared to you. And whether your moment came in your current sport or another one, your task now is to identify the specific identifiable Zone FEEL that you missed or downplayed the first go round.

The telltale feeling in your moment of brilliance is the biggest gift your body has ever given you. By thinking over past memories, you are going to re-experience that feeling, learn to get it back on demand and then experience how it brings out your best performance every time. This is essentially *reverse engineering* and, when you trust what it teaches you, you will have a repeatable Zone:

When I was in the Zone, I got a feeling.

(Reverse Engineering)

Now when I get the feeling, I will get into the Zone

Let's find out how it works.

Exercise: Find Your Zone FEEL

1) Take some time to think about a moment of brilliance. What were you doing? What did you see in that moment? What did you hear? How did you feel? What were you doing physically? Were you playing effortlessly and easily? To the best of your ability, see, hear and feel this experience. As you relive this memory, "go inside" your body and notice your breathing pattern. Is it full and even? Notice the feeling of your spine. Is it upright? Notice your muscles and any other internal sensations in your chest, abdomen or limbs. Make a list of the sensations as demonstrated in the chart.

1st Moment of Brilliance	2nd Moment of Brilliance	3rd Moment of Brilliance
Examples: ☑ Breathing is faster ☑ Posture more erect ☑ Arms and hands light ☑ Chest expansive ☑ Electricity in chest ☑ Abdomen feels solid		

2) Repeat step 1 of this exercise using two more moments of brilliance. Similarly make a list of the sensations for each.

3) Now compare your lists. You are looking for *one sensation* that is common throughout the three experiences. Personally, when I'm in the Zone, I feel an electric sensation in my chest. Clients I've worked with all have their own unique sensations, such as tingling fingers, warm abdomen or relaxed neck. The *ONE*

sensation you choose is your own, so be sure that it is strong, clear and identifiable. Remember the ding of the egg timer — unmistakable.

4) Now close your eyes and identify that sensation in your body. Notice your focus. Notice your posture. Intensify the sensation and feel your adrenaline. This sensation, as you'll soon discover, can create a sense of being unstoppable. And it is now up to you to take it to your game (or the office or school) to experience it.

And that is Zone FEEL — the most important piece of equipment in your arsenal to date. You have reverse-engineered your Zone. So ask yourself: "If I feel this sensation the next time I play, how will I perform?" If the signal typically indicates that you are at your best, trust what it is telling you — and you will be fired up to play exceptionally well.

Chapter Summary

By learning to identify your Zone FEEL, by calling it up on demand and by using it every time you play, you can transform your game. It tells you that you are running optimally right from the get-go. Learn to IDENTIFY and KNOW this feeling. It is your entry point for the Zone. As you move ahead with the system, the real fun will be to maintain it in the face of fierce competition, lousy weather, poor equipment, long tiring days, irritable people, pain and travel. Get used to it; trust it, because there will be days when it is hard to find or sustain. And those days will be gut wrenching — a feeling that is the equally important dark side of the Zone. Read on as the No-Zone FEEL awaits you in the next chapter.

4   Feeling Bad is Good

How performing poorly can teach you so much.

"In great attempts it is glorious even to fail."

— Vince Lombardi, Star Football Coach

When I think back to my competitive years in the martial arts, I had my share of really enjoyable successes but I also had my share of incredibly fabulous losses — yes, fabulous losses. This notion that losses can be useful and that there are benefits to losing often sparks disbelief. How could losing and feeling bad be good? As much as I enjoyed winning — and it was the only reason I was in the game in the first place — losing forced me into many difficult corners that I had to fight my way out of. Each corner proved to be an incredible opportunity to get fed up and quit — or, fight through it and, in the process, develop physical skills, realign mental strategies and test my commitment to my sport.

(I know you are probably tired of hearing that you learn much more from losing than winning. So, instead of leaving you hanging with this advice, I'm going to teach you to get very excited when you lose so that you can wring every last drop out of what it is teaching you — but you'll have to wait for that in Step 3 of the SportExcel System.)

You have now developed your internal signal or Zone FEEL that boldly indicates that you are prepared for battle. With Zone FEEL, there is one and only one thing you notice — the feeling that you can play well, anywhere, anytime. In this chapter, I'm going coin a term — NO Zone — to describe when you fall out of the Zone. With the corresponding NO-Zone FEEL, there is an awareness of sensations that are distinctly opposite and perhaps unpleasant. And there may be many things jumbled in your mind as you are starting to think!

All Olympic-level athletes I've worked with have experienced shifts to the NO-Zone, where they are playing well one moment and struggling the next. In one case, an Olympian described an incident where she lost her Zone FEEL before her match even started. What had happened to her, she wasn't sure, as the only thing she could think of was a teammate saying, "You'll love the targets; I did." Now the comment seems benign (and why it affected her will become apparent in Chapter 20), but by identifying the shift, she was able to take corrective action.

Most of us have experienced this kind of shift — to the No Zone FEEL — our slumped shoulders and frown lines giving it away — as well as the ensuing mistakes. Some of us are in the NO Zone FEEL most of the time and walk around with a cloud over our heads. Worse yet, most of us have no knowledge of what causes it. We have lots of excuses, of course, and you can hear them in your game every day, everything from someone else's fault to lack of sleep. That is why, just as we have a useful signal for the Zone, we need an indicator for the NO Zone: a clear

NO-Zone feeling telling us that — oops — we need to take immediate action or we'll end up in a very unpleasant downward spiral.

Finding Your NO Zone

Most of us have clearly evident NO-Zone sensations that we usually describe as embarrassment, anger, depression, frustration, etc. But we are more interested in the associated unpleasant internal sensations — butterflies, nausea, restricted breathing, sweaty palms, overall heaviness — that reveal just as much as our Zone FEEL — because they are a warning. Yes, they give you a heads-up. And if you can anticipate disaster, you can avoid it. So, just as in the last chapter I had you think of past experiences that "reverse engineered" your Zone, you are going to apply the same process to find a sensation for your NO Zone — a NO-Zone FEEL — so that you can KNOW when you are in danger of going over the cliff and can pull back from the brink.

Exercise: The NO-Zone FEEL

1) Take a moment to think about a moment of disaster, one where you were angry or frustrated, for example, such as with a huge mistake. What were you doing? What did you see in that moment? What did you hear? What did you feel physically when this happened? To the best of your ability, see, hear and feel this experience. As you relive this memory, "go inside" and notice your breathing pattern. Is it restricted? Notice your posture. Is it a bit slumped? Notice your muscles and any other internal sensations in your chest, abdomen or limbs. Make a list of the sensations as demonstrated in the following chart.

1st Moment of Disaster	2nd Moment of Disaster	3rd Moment of Disaster
Examples: ☑ Breathing is tight ☑ Posture is slumped ☑ Arms and hands heavy ☑ Chest hollow ☑ Butterflies in stomach ☑ Chest contracted		

Repeat step 1 of this exercise for two more moments of disaster. Similarly make a list of the sensations.

2) Now compare the experiences. You are looking for *one sensation* that is similar throughout all of your disasters. Personally, I feel butterflies in my gut. Clients I've worked with have their own unique sensations, such as leaden arms, hollow chest, hot face or stiff neck. The *ONE* NO-Zone FEEL you choose is your own personal signal, so be sure it is strong, clear and identifiable.

3) Now, close your eyes and identify that sensation in your body. Notice your focus or lack of it. Notice your self-talk. Notice how you might feel weak, sluggish or heavy. Ask yourself: "If I feel like this when I start my game, how will I perform?" If the answer is: "Terrible," then you are in good company as this represents a very similar sensation to what everyone who loses the Zone feels. This is a very important signal — a head's up to fix some part of your game.

Develop your NO-Zone FEEL

By developing awareness of your NO-Zone FEEL, you will now be able to identify problems with your game before they result in mistakes. As soon as you feel it, you will say, "aha," I know what is happening. It was the person who just said *that* to me. It was *me* watching my teammates melt down. It was *me* listening to the spectators. Now, your NO-Zone FEEL is the means by which you identify and take corrective action *before* your game goes south. The Olympic athlete knew that she needed to take action by her NO-Zone FEEL, even though she missed the original comment that caused it.

So, even in the pressure of a competition, instead of thinking, "Oh no, here we go again," you too will become adept at identifying the shift to the No-Zone. It will tell you much about how certain game-related influences affect your body and your game. And, of course, by the time you finish this book, you will have the ability (a new instinct) to correct the NO-Zone FEEL simply by employing any one of a number of very powerful tools.

Chapter Summary

Get used to the No-Zone FEEL. Become aware of it. Trust it. You need it to be so blatantly obvious that you'll feel sheepish for missing or ignoring it when it results in a mistake, a loss or a disaster. Later, in Step 3, it will become a part of your spectacular high-performance guidance system, so that you learn from both successes and failures. In the next chapter, however, we'll move on to Step 2 — your goals turned into outcomes that seem so real they feel accomplished.

Know and practice your signals before reading on! They are crucial.

Step 2

Outcomes

Leveling the playing field

"Everything is practice."

Pele, Star Soccer Player

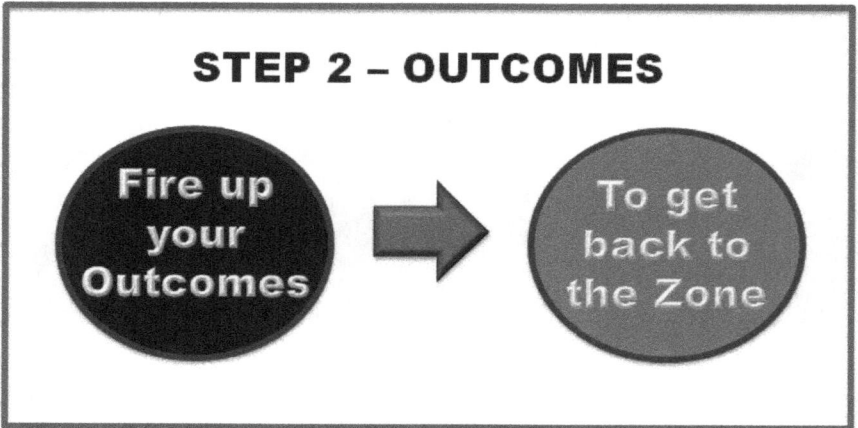

5   Turning Goals into a Done Deal

You know your goals. Now it's time
to supercharge them.

"Don't think about winning. Think about dominating!"

— Pierre Pryor, Star Wrestler and Coach

Within sports there are notable athletes always on the hunt for medals and championships. Somehow they learned to be consistent by way of incredible talent, many hours of training and many hours fighting through vast numbers of competitions. So you ask yourself, can I ever catch up and become as good as they are? And can I possibly do it sooner rather than later? Most things being equal (equipment, coaching and playing time), in this chapter I am going to show you how you can begin to level the playing field by putting in extra practice time and competing in hundreds of additional competitions — at no cost and minimal time — just by processing your goals a bit differently and seeing them as "done deals" or outcomes.

This is Step 2 of the SportExcel System for high performance. You are going to go on a training regimen where much of your training will be done in your head through a process I call DÉJÀ-VU DVD, because athletes who have won many times over KNOW they'll do it again — no thinking, no doubt. And you need to be just like them when you compete — no thinking, no doubt. With DÉJÀ-VU DVD, you will experience your outcome of winning just like a professional, World Champion or Olympian. When your game starts with such a strong sense of KNOWING, success feels like a foregone conclusion.

DÉJÀ-VU DVD Guidelines

DÉJÀ-VU DVD uses what is often called visualization or guided imagery or game rehearsal. But there is more — a physical component that is so subtle you sometimes miss it. But you'll feel it. And, when you do it properly, you'll feel like you are playing your game in living color with the smells of locker room sweat, where you are totally in the moment and "at one" with your equipment. Oh, and you'll get to experience what it feels like to be on the podium, holding the cup and looking at all those adorning fans.

Most importantly, you'll actually feel micro-muscle movements, a process that I've coined "physicalization," based on some work I've done with Olympic athletes who expect competitions to feel the same as their rehearsals. The ultimate aim with any visualization or physicalization is to rehearse your goals so precisely that you begin to feel that you have already been to the competition, gotten the T-shirt and WON. Hence, DÉJÀ VU.

Here are the rules of "DÉJÀ-VU DVD-ing":

1) Know what you want. What does winning mean to you? Will you be on the podium? Top five, 10 or other? Will you make the tryout? Sign the contract? Know these things and the resulting DEJA-VU DVD practice session will be easy, precise and empowering. And remember to include the podium, medal, victory dance or other celebration. It is why you participate in competitive sport, end of story.

2) Be engaged. I was working with a young ski racer who was reluctant to follow the DÉJÀ-VU DVD process, mostly because his coach had taught him another way. I asked him to take a moment and visualize his most recent race as an example. He closed his eyes for several seconds and when he reopened them, I told him that he had crashed. He looked at me wide-eyed as if to say, how did you know? I knew because he went from sitting upright in the chair to being slightly slumped. His body said it all; he was disengaged from the Zone or the feeling of success.

How you practice DÉJÀ-VU DVD is how you will perform, fully engaged, or not. In Chapter 22, I'll discuss the importance of managing your adrenaline levels so that you can have a steady supply at the start and throughout the competition. In the meantime, you'll need to get acquainted with your adrenaline so that you can use plenty of it in your DÉJÀ-VU DVD practice session, before you get anywhere near your sports venue.

3) Create the feeling of déjà vu. Create the feeling of having been there many times before. The more often you do DÉJÀ-VU DVD practice, the more comfortable you will get in competition.

I used DÉJÀ-VU DVD to help me rehearse for my black belt karate tournaments in the kata, or forms component, which is a combination of dance, fighting technique, bar brawl, athleticism and over-the-top energy. Before utilizing this approach, the smallest mistakes in my form, perhaps not even discernable to the judges, would get me thinking and trigger the NO Zone. A mere eight weeks later in the ring — which is plenty of time to rehearse the Zone using DÉJÀ-VU DVD but not enough to correct all imperfections — the head judge was in front of me flipping his score cards with the same intensity that I had displayed in the ring. I was in the Zone, and he'd felt it. I'd surely made some mistakes; yet I got the highest score I'd ever received. Eight weeks, seven days each week, three times a day — I'd won that event more than 168 times in my head and it was a moment that nothing could derail.

4) Build your skills. DÉJÀ-VU DVD is a skill-building process, where you build skills in both your technique and your general performance. While this kind of rehearsal is not a substitute for playing your game, it greatly enhances regular practice and in many cases it will help you to resolve flaws in routines and to practice in conditions that would be hard to create, such as windstorms or torrid heat. You can also save huge sums of money by this kind of rehearsal as there is no venue to rent. More importantly, what you learn in competition can be applied to your DEJA VU DVD practice so that you can continually narrow the gap between what you want and where you currently are at in your sport.

Exercise: DÉJÀ-VU DVD

DÉJÀ-VU DVD takes advantage of the brain's incredible capacity to rehearse an upcoming event, both visually and physically. As you do this exercise, understand that your idea of visualization may be quite different from my version or that of your teammates. Some will see images in living color, some will see hazy shades of black and white and some see absolutely nothing, even though they seem to know the precise details of the successful event that they are viewing.

Step 1: Visualization.

a) Sit in a comfortable chair in a room away from distractions.

b) Close your eyes and in your mind see a DVD player and TV in front of you. In your hand, you hold the DVD of your upcoming competition. The name of the event and the date are transcribed in bold letters on the disk. This is a recording of your future. Insert the disk into the imaginary DVD player and turn on the TV. As you watch your performance in your mind, be amazed by your incredible skill and poise. Note how much fun you are having. Sit on the edge of your seat as you watch and FEEL YOUR ADRENALINE and Zone FEEL. I repeat, sit on the edge of your seat as you watch and FEEL YOUR ADRENALINE and Zone FEEL. If you are doing this right, you will look very silly so find a spot away from family or spectators.

c) Watch the entire event (or just parts of it), the joys of the successes and especially the amazing recovery after your mistakes. Play the DVD for as long as you like.

Step 2: Physicalization

a) Now, in your mind, step up into your image on the screen, so that you become the person you've been watching. From this vantage point, notice all the people around you, from competitors to officials. Then play the game as you want to play it.

b) Continue and experience your Zone FEEL. Feel your adrenaline and enjoy.

c) Step off the screen, remove the DVD and note the date on it. This is your future. Place the DVD in your "back pocket" and pull it out daily to mentally watch and rehearse your success.

And that is it — short and sweet — or as long as you want to make it. I encourage you to do DÉJÀ-VU DVD at least once a day — both the visualization and the physicalization components. For elite athletes, pros and Olympians, play yours several times a day and get comfortable with your performance. If you practice in the evening, there may come a time when your adrenaline will kick in so quickly and powerfully that you'll find some difficulty getting to sleep afterward. At this point, pat yourself on the back for connecting your adrenaline to your game and reschedule DÉJÀ-VU DVD practice to the morning or afternoon.

Chapter Summary

Using DÉJÀ-VU DVD gives you the same advantage that all elite athletes have. They know that they are going to perform well before they get anywhere near the game. At the outset, ensure you have a quiet place to watch your DVD. After a while, you'll find the training effective even in noisy airport waiting areas and on the plane itself.

Watch your DVD and enjoy the feeling of confidence it gives you, as it enables you to rehearse both your skills and your Zone. Become the high performance champion of your dreams in the comfort of your own chair. You'll save time, save money and learn to play with passion. In the next chapter, we'll look at an example of how DÉJÀ-VU DVD is used in a sport situation.

6 Creating Déjà Vu Requires Practice

Mental rehearsal and physical rehearsal are opposite sides of the same coin.

"You cannot discover new oceans unless you have the courage to lose sight of the other shore."

— Anonymous, Star Genius

From karate to track and field, using DÉJÀ-VU DVD in Step 2 of this system helps you acquire and fine-tune your skills to compete at the highest levels. Having worked with several sports, I'll give you an example of the DÉJÀ-VU DVD process from the point of view of a sport that may be far removed from yours — snowboarding. It will give you a sense of how you can accelerate your learning curve and practice winning in your head as opposed to on the field, court, pool, etc.

I have always enjoyed skiing without being competitive and without having to imagine being a high performance racer. However, a friend observed me skiing and said I had all the balance and finesse of a hockey player who needed something to hit. It was, she said, the kind of finesse that classy skiers avoided being associated with (partly for safety reasons). However, she agreed to swallow her pride and teach me some of the finer points.

Over the next two skiing seasons, she encouraged me to "step into her shoes" and model her style and technique as I followed her down the hill. She gave me specific pointers and showed me how to plant my ski poles, which, up to then, had been only useful, I thought, for skewering fellow skiers as I awkwardly got on or off the lift. At times I felt fabulous, at times scared, and most of the time I felt like I was going way too fast. So, on the many trips up the lift, I visualized and physicalized competent athletic sweeps across and down the hill.

Stretch Yourself

Knowing that I was a karate instructor, my friend turned the tables on me and gave me levels of success — yellow belt to start and progressing upward — grading me like I grade my karate students. I liked the approach as it gave me outcomes to strive for. Eventually, two years from that first lesson, I started to feel comfortable and a little classy myself — perhaps a skiing brown belt — as my speeds were faster but felt slower. So I was not prepared when she cornered me on the lift and said, in a matter of fact, not to be argued with voice: "Let's take up snowboarding next year."

My heart nearly stopped. "Are you crazy?" I wanted to say. But, being male, I said, "Sure, why not?"

Ouch. My backside already began to hurt just thinking about snowboarding. I even plugged the thought into a DÉJÀ-VU DVD and my initial attempts made me feel queasy and produced a disquieting array of images of bumping down the hill, slinky-like, mostly on my backside, sometimes on my head. I'd never really felt panic before with sports, not even in karate. Snowboarding was different. My DVD of being strapped to a "plank," helmeted and wrist splinted, and going headlong down a mountain felt awkward and life threatening.

My saving grace, I suppose, is the career that I follow and my ability to walk my talk. If I can get athletes to overcome fear, I thought, I can do it for myself — I hoped. I'd watched a lot of snowboarding at the winter Olympics in 2010 — keeping tabs on Hannah Teter with whom I'd worked — so I had amazing snowboarding images in my head — the world's best as examples. I went back to the DÉJÀ-VU DVD process and pretended to be them. I had my doubts (probably because of my allergy to pain) but within about five minutes of DÉJÀ-VU DVD practice I was able to imagine myself sweeping across the hill. It was cool.

Taking it to the next level, I attempted to carve (which means to weave gracefully back and forth in an S pattern), but that still eluded me and evoked the queasiness. And that's where I sit as I write this. However, I'm persisting. And each day I practice DÉJÀ-VU DVD, I expect the queasiness to grow fainter. My goal is to practice in this manner, so that when winter comes and I am strapped into a snowboard, my progress will be effortless and, more importantly, painless!

Exercise: DÉJÀ-VU TWO

As I'm discovering, no sport or aspect of a sport is too complicated (or scary) for the DÉJÀ-VU DVD process. Give it a try yourself and experiment with the following exercise.

1) Start by feeling adrenaline surging in your veins, and, of course, establish your Zone FEEL.

2) With both sensations, visualize yourself in an emotionally charged situation such as a playoff or sudden-death situation. See yourself in action, larger than life, calmer than calm, outrageously competent, highly successful. (I like to see myself "ten feet tall" and glowing.)

3) Now, make the experience physical — play after play. This *IS* training, so have yourself make an occasional mistake just so you can overcome it — without missing a beat. Put yourself in all kinds of conditions, just to get your body and brain used to what you may face in competition.

4) Next, take it a step further and (just as I challenged myself in snowboarding) transform the difficult parts of your game by seeing yourself comparable to pros or Olympians — one, two or even 20 different ones — until it feels good to go toe-to-toe with them in your visualization and you can maintain your Zone FEEL as you do it.

Visualizing *IS* practice. It helps you get started as a beginner; it helps you to build confidence and consistency; and it helps you to overcome any number of problematic parts of your game. You already have many images of excellence in your head. Utilize them and make DÉJÀ-VU DVD practice a daily part of your practice regimen, particularly before training sessions and competitions. And, as most sports are expensive, it can help you to elevate your game in a shorter time with less expense.

Chapter Summary

My snowboarding DÉJÀ-VU DVD practice will eventually be put to the test, and my current anxiety level reveals a lot more work still needs to be done. However, when you know your outcome and know beforehand what it will look and feel like, you'll have a much greater chance of getting it done. Any way you look at it, the quest for the Zone starts with your ability to get excited by your future. In the next chapter we'll set up some parameters around DÉJÀ-VU DVD practice to further enhance your chances of winning.

7   More Than Just Winning!

Winning is a nice way of living life to the fullest;
so is having friends. Both can be mutually inclusive.

"Love the game. Love the game for the pure joy of accomplishment.
Love the game for everything it can teach you about yourself.
Love the game for the feeling of belonging to a group endeavoring
to do its best.
Love the game for being involved in a team whose members
can't wait to see you do your best.
Love the game for the challenge of working harder than you ever have
at something and then harder than that.
Love the game because it takes all team members to give it life.
Love the game because at its best, the game tradition
will include your contribution.
Love the game because you belong to a long line of fine athletes
who have loved it. It is now your legacy.
Love the game so much that you will pass on your love of the game to
another athlete who has seen your dedication, your work,
your challenges, your triumphs... and then that athlete will,
because of you, love the game."

— Anonymous, Star Motivator

S everal years ago, I was working with a young athlete who had an awful experience at a major U.S. event. He is a very capable athlete and especially adept at using what his coaches and my system have taught him. But in a session prior to a major competition, he told me he was going to win for his family and community, as they were helping him raise money for his training. I almost stopped him on the spot so that he could further explain this outcome, but I held my tongue. I figured it would be a good experience for him to discover how being focused on the wrong outcome could be counterproductive. For example, one can set the goal to be rich, but reaching that goal by robbing banks can cause problems.

Careful What You Wish For

Being totally focused on the outcome of winning — for love or money — is fraught with similar pitfalls. It can become an unhealthy obsession that may blind us to problematic behaviors. It can also obscure the ethical side of sport where performance-enhancing drugs may appear justified. And it can create a "win at all costs" mentality by which other deviousness gets played out.

Coaches can also be caught in this trap as sometimes they will play favorites with their own athletes, especially those who are most fulfilling to work with. And it makes sense. These athletes learn the fastest, take on responsibility and leadership and make the coach look good by winning. Hence, they will often get most of the coach's attention (even though the coach may not be aware of this). Coaches who get caught in this trap can even unintentionally undermine the rest of their athletes.   I believe that most coaches would be in denial and be truly appalled if this were pointed out to them.   Quite simply, they have muddied their outcome of winning with that of desiring to coach their athletes equally.

Going for the win as an athlete has similar pitfalls.   Golfers who cheat and get caught may refuse to acknowledge their behavior.   Even if the illegal act were caught on camera, they may be unable to see the error of their ways.   When you set the outcome to win, it gets wired in, and the subconscious mind takes over and strange things can happen.   People who never cheat will cheat, and they are hard-pressed to be convinced that they did wrong because they have been raised in good homes where cheating is something only bad guys do.

The young athlete I mentioned earlier had a different problem with his outcome of winning — called losing.   He loved his parents and community sponsors and greatly appreciated their financial support in his quest for success.   He believed that winning honored their support and, by default, losing dishonored it.   What an incredible burden for any athlete to carry.

I can think of many athletes who have won world championships and then faltered in an Olympic year when their country's honor was at stake. (Some athletes, of course, do just the opposite.)   The national audience is watching for the first time and there is an ongoing tally of the country's self-worth as measured by the medals.

I've been asked, "Isn't going for the prize and the glory everyone's outcome?"   It may be — but that's only a part of it.   There are a wealth of other components that can give perspective and balance. There has to be, or why would so many athletes bother to come back year after year to the competitions when there are only a few winners?

When setting outcomes for competitions, I encourage athletes to start with their dream of winning the big prize. Then I get them to enrich the experience by stepping back and creating sub-outcomes that will ultimately support that dream. I ask one simple question of every athlete: "If you were to have fun and be in the Zone for the whole competition, how would you do?" The answer is usually "I'd do well." This is the first complementary outcome to winning: *Stay in the Zone*.

Sub-outcomes for Success

There are five sub-outcomes you can set when you are heading to a competition. When you can succeed in all five, you will be learning how to support the main outcome of winning and have a great experience as a bonus.

1) Establish and learn Zone FEEL. You have already learned this. If not, go back to Chapter 3. It *IS* that important.

2) Get excited by mistakes, losses and emotional collapses. They will happen, so you might as well learn from them. Competitions give you an incredible opportunity to learn and improve your game by fixing the fallout. By the time you finish this book you will have quite the tool kit with which to do this.

3) Act on everything that happens to you. It is all good. In Step 3 of the SportExcel System we'll develop this further, as each time you make any correction or fix any problem, it goes into your

mental data bank and builds the resolute, competitive skills that go beyond your conscious mind. In my years of martial arts competition I ultimately learned more from my losses than I did from my victories. (I did appreciate my victories however. They were sweet.)

4) Perceive the world as a friendly place where everything works to your advantage. When it is windy, you love wind. When it is rainy, you love rain. When the officials are cranky, you love to get them on your side. When you have to play against the best athletes or teams in the county, state, province, country or world, you love the challenge and any attempts to intimidate you.

5) Enjoy the friends and coaches you meet at competitions. An "osmosis" learning effect takes place at competitions: what you learn from these relationships cannot be taught in practice. You also can enjoy the exotic locations, the travel, the opportunity to represent your club, town or country, the scenery and the mementoes. These experiences will make you a better athlete, create memories that will last a lifetime and keep you coming back.

Chapter Summary

When you flesh out your "outcome to win" with the five sub-outcomes you will continue to grow in your abilities; you will make incredible life-long coaching and competitive allies; you will be well respected outside of competition and feared within it; you will become a student of the game; and you will honor everyone who knows you. It is also the path to consistency and achieving your dream of winning. By setting up proper outcomes in Step 2, you will learn the path to the Zone in all aspects of competition — AND I BELIEVE YOU WILL ULTIMATELY HAVE A MUCH GREATER CHANCE OF WINNING. In the next chapter, I'll encourage you to keep your outcomes very specific.

8 Covering All of the Bases

Now that you're wildly excited about the prospects for the
new season, you'll need to dig a little deeper
and work on specifics.

"Nothing is particularly hard if you divide it into small jobs."

— Henry Ford, Star Entrepreneur

At season's end, athletes in all sports need to take a break to rest and recuperate, whether your previous year was wildly successful, or not. Then, as the new season dawns, you'll be rested and healthy, having recovered from the aches and pains of a grueling year. And you'll be excitedly gnawing on the bit with all manner of possibilities for the adventure that lies ahead in the new season.

These possibilities are your true starting point of the season, and now is the time to write them down as outcomes for your year. These outcomes project what you want to achieve — in a checklist fashion — so that you'll know month by month if you are achieving them and making any progress in your game. Aw, you might say, but I'm only a recreational athlete and setting specific outcomes makes recreational sports sound like work. Well, it does, and it is work, but only at the beginning of the season. Once you get into full stride, it will make your season easier because setting your outcomes puts the responsibility for your season fully in your hands. Here are your choices:

1) You can have your colleagues — some who may be very negative and disruptive — set outcomes for you;

2) You can allow your subconscious mind — with all its negative self-talk and minor phobias — to set outcomes for you; or,

3) You can set them consciously.

Outcomes are going to happen and it is just a matter of how, and by whom, they get set.

When I was a young athlete I set no outcomes, not consciously at least, although my dream was to play hockey in the National Hockey League someday. For me, the only other goal I knew had mesh, was framed in steel, and was where I had to get the puck. Even as a high school football player, I set no outcomes. In recreational sports such as tennis, squash, badminton and table tennis, I set no outcomes. Karate, as I remember it, was the only sport where I set outcomes, but the sport was laid out in an outcome-oriented progression of belt levels. For tournaments, however, my outcomes were about not losing, versus what I really wanted, winning. As I mentioned earlier, I changed that around pretty quickly with the DÉJÀ-VU DVD exercise.

If this sways you to get serious about outcome setting, the first thing you need to do is to specifically define your outcomes for the year. You need to write down your outcomes — exactly as you want them to unfold —— as part as part of a training plan with regard to technique training, physical training (which includes healthy eating), mental training and tournament experience. If this sounds like a plan for an Olympic development team, it is, but it is also for you.

The process is straightforward and can produce incredible results, both in your game and in your life. Outcomes such as cross training and striving for efficiency of movement can certainly improve your stamina over the season of competing, help you to feel better, and, perhaps get your coach to sit up and take notice.

An outcome such as improving your technique can introduce you to new ideas and help you become a student of the game. An outcome such as improving your mental game can give you a personal calmness and consistency and ability to bring out the best in yourself and others. And an outcome such as enjoying competition can build a sense of wellbeing like nothing you can imagine. So, set your outcomes for your competitive year in these categories — physical training, technical training, mental training and competing, then find the resources to support this training.

Physical Training

The physical training will involve anything from walking to jogging to running to cycling to swimming, to name just a few. Of course, take into consideration the normal disclaimer that you need to consult your physician if you are starting from scratch or have weight or health challenges. Be specific as to how much exercise you are going to do and write the times down on a weekly schedule. Start with fewer reps and move to higher repetitions. Set your outcomes so that your workout follows a plan and is time limited. That way you won't quit early — unless you feel ill — and you won't extend it, even if you feel fantastic. Set it up in this way and you'll find a greater success in staying committed to your outcome.

Technical Training

Technical training should involve a coach so that you have a training system and a way of getting feedback on your technique. Otherwise, you may be practicing incorrect techniques over and over so that future coaching corrections will be much more difficult. With your practice outcomes, set the amount of time and lay out a plan for your training. Ask your coach to give you specific drills. Write out your plan and go from drill to drill, ending with a competition style round or some other fun activity. Stick with your plan and stick with your time allotment. Completing your plan sets you up for success. Pat yourself on the back. Learn to enjoy success.

Mental Training

Your mental training is ongoing and continues throughout your physical training, technical training and competition. Set outcomes around the amount of time you will spend on this. It is said that sport is 90 percent mental and 10 percent physical, but you'd never spend 90 percent of your time training mentally. However, you can invert the ratio and spend 10 percent on mental training and 90 percent on physical and technical training as the mind can compress a whole lot of mental practice into a short period of time. In five minutes of mental work, I can golf several rounds of golf, very effectively and very inexpensively — WITH ADRENALINE. The exercises I'm presenting in the following chapters will give you plenty of mental work to do, but you may also benefit from additional tools from a high performance expert.

Competition Training

Lastly, you want to craft some outcomes around how you want to compete. Competing involves a whole different skillset and a whole different set of outcomes to support it. You need to be able to respond to efforts to undermine or intimidate you. You need to love putting yourself on the line and treat competition like a friend. You need to be flexible and to be able to recover quickly from mistakes. You need to know how much time you expect to stay in the Zone and where you will finish as part of the team or in individual sport. It is important to spend some time setting these kinds of outcomes as all the practice and all the technical skill in the world can come to naught under the spotlight of competition.

Mileposts with the Scorecard

Of course, all of these areas need to be evaluated from time to time over your season and modified if necessary or changed as you complete your outcomes, but, most importantly, you have to write them down at the outset. I've provided a very simple example of a countdown chart on page 55 that you can use as a template to create your own chart on a single sheet of paper or on the computer. At a glance you'll be able to see how your year will unfold, with the year-end month AT THE TOP and working downward to the start of your year AT THE BOTTOM. This may seem odd to you but I encourage you to do it this way so that the first thing you always see is where you want to get to by the end of your season. It is nice, neat and tidy and at a glance you can see the path you are going to take. And, when an outcome is completed, you check it off. So, if you haven't already done so, set your outcomes for your season now — even if the season has already started.

Chapter Summary

Start gnawing on the bit for each sports adventure that lies ahead. In preparation, write down the indicators of how you will perform. Once you do, you'll be headed in a direction where your technical skills will be strong, your body fit, your mind flexible and you'll perform like nobody is watching in your quest to learn how to win. In the next chapter we'll look at Step 3 of the SportExcel System to understand the incredible guidance you get when outcomes go wrong — the bad and the ugly of your game. It is your ability to understand that mistakes and disasters are merely GPS or guidance, as they will teach you much, much more than your successes.

Be capable of transforming your goals into outcomes before moving on.

Month	Coundown Chart Outcomes **Karate Outcomes Example** Goals related to skill, enjoyment, events, dietary regimen, strength, fitness, routine, etc.	✔
Sept (The end of your season)	National Competition/championship — top five or better 100% Zone FEEL Taper to competition -- optimum weight – running twice per week Visualization daily Practice at dojo 2 times per week and 1 time at home Only eat healthy foods and maintain optimum weight Technique well-oiled and smooth	
Aug	6th regional competition – win the competition, live in Zone FEEL and have fun Running 3 X per week — lose final 2 lbs. Visualization daily Maintain home practice Practice at club 2 X per week Healthy eating	
July	5th regional competition – win and have fun Running 4 X per week — lose 8 of 10 pounds — healthy eating Visualization daily Maintain home practice and club practice Healthy eating	
June	4th regional competition – Place and have fun Running walking and maintain exercise — lose 6 of 10 pounds —only healthy eating choices Visualization daily Learn specific techniques Maintain home practice and club practice	
May	3rd competition -- have fun, stay in the Zone, experiment Daily Running and maintain exercise — lose 6 of 10 pounds — only healthy eating choices Visualization daily Learn specific techniques Maintain home practice and club practice	
April	2nd competition — have fun, stay in the Zone, experiment Daily running and maintain exercise — lose 4 of 10 pounds —consistent healthy eating choices Visualization daily Learn specific techniques for competition Practice at club	
March	1st competition (have fun, stay in the Zone, use result as guidance) Daily running and increase exercise — lose 2 of 10 pounds —consistent healthy eating choices Visualization to daily Learn specific new techniques for competition Practice at club	
Feb	Practice at club — relax have fun Start visualization of specific outcomes Continue a healthy eating plan	
Jan	Practice at club — relax have fun Start visualization of specific outcomes Continue a healthy eating plan	
Dec	Practice at club — relax have fun, move up intensity Start visualization of specific outcomes Start a healthy eating plan	
Nov	Practice at club — relax and have fun	
Oct (The beginning of your season)	Take time off and enjoy time off!!!!!!!	

Step 3

GPS

That lousy match really taught me a lesson — not.

"Slump? I ain't in no slump - I just ain't hitting."

— *Yogi Berra, Star Baseball Player*

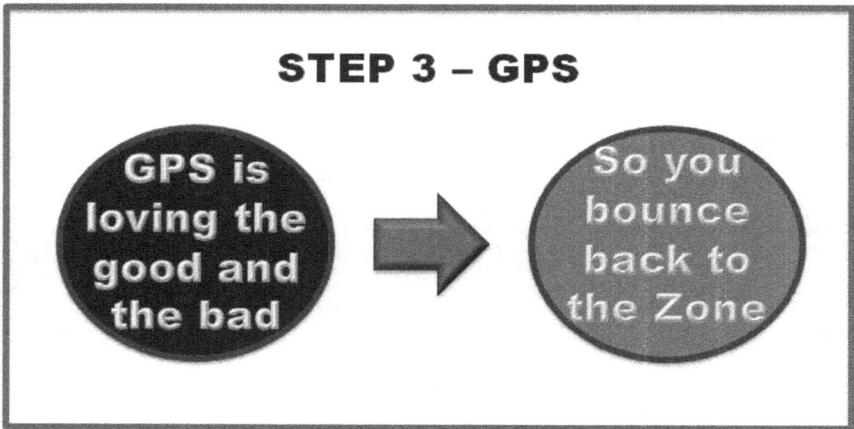

STEP 3 – GPS

GPS is loving the good and the bad ➡ So you bounce back to the Zone

9   **Guided by GPS**

Learning like a perfectionist — and loving it.

"Learning without thought is wasted labor; thought without learning is perilous."

— *Confucius, Star Philosopher*

"Learning is not compulsory...neither is survival."

— *W. Edwards Deming, Star Statistician*

"Let your heart guide you. It whispers, so listen closely."

— *Anonymous, Star Poet*

When the quarter, period, inning, game, season, etc. is over, it is time for reflection. And whether you've had a great quarter, period, inning, game, season, etc. or one to forget, it is very important to assess where you went right and where you could still improve. I've worked with some of the best athletes in the world and they, in particular, are always looking for the edge that this kind of reflection gives them.

So what makes elite athletes look to the past to overcome their limitations? Partly it is called being a perfectionist, which in my opinion is a requirement for any athlete to be great. Being a perfectionist means that you are always looking for new ways to help you to win, whereas a "who cares" kind of athlete is merely along for the ride. And what makes perfectionists tick is their awareness of something I call GPS, a suck-it-up kind of response to adversity that helps them identify the gaps between their current (sometimes nasty) reality and the perfection that they have created via their dreams.

Susan, the GPS Lady

The real GPS — Global Positioning System — is a satellite-based, radio-wave, triangulation system that allows your GPS unit in your car to accurately figure out where you are. Updated constantly, it uses satellite radio beams to pinpoint your movements and to give you guidance on a computer-generated map. The GPS device in my car is a she — Susan — and she guides me wherever I ask her to take me. And most of the time she is sweet.

Now the point of this is that Susan helps me make corrections with the greatest of ease in territory unknown to me. Most of time we have a wonderful relationship and I accept her guidance willingly and happily and I greatly benefit from it especially on foggy nights in unfamiliar cities.

When on occasion I do get angry with her, like the time we had a pitched battle when I was driving into New York State from Ontario, Canada, I learned that she sometimes defaults to factory settings, such as *non-expressway mode*. I'm sure I saw every side street in Buffalo, NY until

I finally stopped and figured Susan out and safely got to my destination. So the anger — as good as it felt to let off steam — was unwarranted as following her guidance helps me to get to my destination quickly, efficiently, stress free and (mostly) tantrum free, even when technology works less efficiently than I would like.

GPS is a Mixed Bag

In a manner similar to how technology guides you in your car, you have your own internal GPS guidance system that is guiding you on your road to high performance and success. When you experience bad scores, long-term diminished stats, plain misfortune or emotions such as frustration, anger and disappointment, they can be the "end of the earth for you" in terms of emotional fallout, or you can use them as guidance to identify and correct what they are telling you as you make progress toward your outcome.

This internal GPS gives you a huge opportunity to improve your game. Losses and mistakes offer you some pretty immediate and accurate GPS guidance. It *is* guidance — much like "MAKE AN IMMEDIATE U-TURN!" is guidance from Susan. And it is very important for you to understand how your internal GPS works, so that you can use it to identify problems and constructively take corrective action *before* your game goes south. Because even the "ugly" experiences can benefit you.

The Athlete Who Acted Like He'd Won

A young athlete called me on my cellphone while my wife and I were out walking our dog. I permit all my athletes to call me during post-business-day times, but only in special "Olympic-type" situations. In his case, he was playing in the first big game of the season against the team that was expected to win the division. I figured that could qualify.

I was expecting it to be a pregame call, and this call was post game, and that was surprising. He told me that he had great news, even though his team had lost the game. (He had lost but still he had great news. That was definitely a new concept for him.) He apologized for bothering me and talked quickly, describing how they had gotten behind in points right from the get-go, but that he had persevered and stayed in his Zone — overcoming the urge to quit (GPS). And when his teammates slumped and tried to give up (GPS), he fired them up and got them back in the game (GPS). Even after throwing an interception, he still managed to maintain his Zone (GPS).

Further, he told me that they had clawed their way back to within a touchdown and only a dropped pass in the dying seconds had ended the comeback — and that he still felt fantastic about the result (GPS). But there was more, he said. He had also kicked a couple of fabulous punts. And there was even more, he said; a scout from a college had pulled him aside to speak with him after the game. (You could imagine the scout's response if he *had* quit.)

The Only Way to Learn

This was one happy football player who had just lost a game. And if you are fiercely competitive like him, every time you overcome adversity — a single mistake or a disastrous game — you build your skillset in incredible ways. And every time you break through frustration, anger, and pain; or learn a new skill; or deal effectively with teammates losing motivation; or make the spectators, wind, cold or noise disappear, you have utilized your internal GPS and have likely improved your game immeasurably.

The guidance you get from your internal GPS is the very powerful Step 3 of the SportExcel System. This third step, GPS, is the understanding that you must embrace the good, bad and ugly of your game as the ONLY way to improve your performance. Add that to your feel of the Zone (Step 1) and your ability to create adrenalized outcomes (Step 2), and you have *everything* to get excited about.

Chapter Summary

The young football player was aware of the No-Zone, sinking feeling when behind in points, and he learned to feel it as an indication to continue moving forward. That kind of internal GPS, similar to the version in your car, just feels good, especially for a perfectionist who likes tangible evidence that his or her game is moving forward. And it also warms the hearts of others who see you developing character and performing well. And warmth in their hearts, well, that sounds a lot like Zone FEEL — the kind of GPS that we'll explore further in the next chapter.

10 The Signal Says Go For It

The Zone Signal is fantastic GPS — The secret weapon in your arsenal.

"Most athletes stop when they begin to tire. Good athletes go until they think they are going to collapse. But the very best know the mind tires before the body, and push themselves further and further, beyond all limits. Only when their limits are shattered can the attainable be reached."

— Mark Mysnyk, Star Collegiate Wrestler
[as edited by Bob Palmer]

I believe that in sport, there are no winners or losers, only those who actively participate in guiding their mindset with regard to their outcomes, and those who leave it to chance (or to others). When I watch any professional sport, it usually takes me one look at the posture of the coach and athletes during a game to know whether they are either winning or losing. Unfortunately, for most athletes, *The Game* runs their lives instead of them running *The Game*.

The Game can be like a two-year-old. It cooperates or throws a tantrum, or more than likely swings back and forth between cooperation and war. Would you let a toddler run your life at the grocery checkout demanding and grabbing for the box of candy bars until he got one? Not likely. But if you allow yourself to get embarrassed by the other shoppers' impatience, you might succumb to the pressure and lose your cool (aka the Zone).

In the same manner many of us let our game get away from us until it runs our lives — embarrassment from others watching our mistakes, frustration that the new equipment performs poorly, anger that the new skills still need practice. We need to take charge and tame *The Game* by staying with the Zone feeling you learned in the previous chapters. Stay in charge of your Zone and *The Game* — win or lose — will take care of itself and allow magic to happen. This is Step 3 in the SportExcel System — using GPS-like guidance of your Zone and No-Zone FEEL to manage your high performance game, guiding you just as effectively as your car's GPS device guides your trip.

Practical Use of the Zone and NO-Zone FEEL

You now have acquired clear signals for being in the Zone — Zone FEEL — and for being in the NO-Zone — NO-Zone FEEL. These signals give you the clear GPS guidance you need as you move toward to your DÉJÀ-VU DVD-empowered and inspired outcomes. The following example will give you an idea of how it works.

Imagine yourself at a traffic light in a busy metropolitan area. The light turns red, yet you force yourself to go through. If you are like most people, you'll feel an internal sensation (a No-Zone FEEL) that says DANGER or STOP or LOOK FOR A POLICE OFFICER or AM I INSANE? That is your signal telling you that something is wrong.

Now, imagine yourself back at the traffic light as it turns green — and go through. My guess is that you felt an entirely different sensation, one that said THIS IS OKAY, where you feel relaxed and at ease. You might check to the left and right before entering the imaginary intersection, but your internal sensation said, "GO." That is your signal telling you that everything is alright.

That is how your Zone sensations act as your GPS system, in much the same way the GPS device in your car guides you through the city. Feel the NO-Zone FEEL and you know you have to fix something. Experience the Zone FEEL and trust that everything is a go. Translate that to the game, and your body's instant relay of Zone or NO-Zone messages will guide you to the Zone every time and help you stay there. What could be simpler?

The Need to be Ready

Many athletes and teams have an expectation that they can work their way into the Zone, hole by hole, inning by inning or quarter by quarter. That was my expectation when I played hockey as a young athlete. Sometimes it worked, because in hockey a team can play dismally for two periods and then they find the Zone and win the game. But when I competed in the martial arts it was a different story. In less than a minute I could be out of the competition after traveling at great expense and time. That is where I learned the importance of being in the Zone from the outset. My Zone FEEL signal — warmth in my chest — usually told me that at the start. It was brilliant and very comfortable GPS.

When we travel through a major urban area, we are guided by not one, but many traffic lights. We stop on red, go on green and proceed with extreme caution on amber. Except for rush hour, the system works pretty well. Now imagine if all the traffic lights are cloaked on our side of the intersection and the only way for us to tell if they are red, green or amber is to proceed through the intersection and look in the rearview mirror. It would be very scary and life threatening. Soon every intersection would produce anxiety and fear and we'd be stuck — too scared to move.

And yet that is how many of us compete. We step nervously onto the ice, field, court, etc. — red light equivalent — and somehow expect to perform well. Feeling bad (nervous, tight, fearful, etc.) before we start is like anticipating a collision at every intersection. On the other hand, being worried throughout a game (and only feeling our Zone FEEL with a victory) is like looking in the rearview mirror at the end of the game to see that the light *was* green and we were worrying needlessly. The purpose of having our Zone FEEL is to guide us to success *before* entering the competitive "intersections" of our sport.

When you feel your Zone FEEL (green light), you know to go for it. When you feel your NO-Zone FEEL (red light) you know to fix whatever the problem is so that you get your Zone back — and then proceed. Thus far in this book — to set up this GPS system and to guide you properly — you have been challenged to develop your Zone and NO-Zone sensations to the point where they are as distinct and useful as traffic lights. If you have yet to do so and are reading this book as you would a novel, please go back and do this piece of homework. It is the foundation of this system.

When I first learned to play golf, I wanted to impress my partners and anyone else who might be watching. I was nervous, and hoped the ball would go where I wanted it to go. I flailed away at it and, when it travelled to the proper destination, I took my imagined bow to the onlookers. On the other hand, a professional golfer KNOWS where the ball is going to go. He feels his Zone FEEL before he steps up to it. If he hears someone talk or click a camera, he may lose that feeling and step back to shake off the NO-Zone FEEL. Once he feels his Zone FEEL, he knows he is back on track — GPS.

That is the important point to be made here and the only way to play any sport. Being in the Zone dramatically increases the odds that you will be engaging every one of your skills, every component of your physiology and all your senses. By doing so, you engage the pleasant feeling, make your competitors mentally disappear, embrace all kinds of weather, accept your equipment and trust your preparedness. You are in the NOW; you are ready to perform; and you have a way of KNOWING you will be successful. The light is green.

Exercise: Shifting between Zone and NO-Zone FEEL

1) Stand in front of a mirror and think of a negative memory of a competition that produces the NO-Zone FEEL. Stay in the memory for about twenty seconds and become aware of your breathing, your posture, and other internal sensations. Look at

yourself in the mirror. Notice your facial muscles, your eyes, your jaw and other external features. Not a pretty sight, I imagine.

2) Now, think of an experience that produces your Zone FEEL. Get fully into this memory. Notice how your posture starts to shift along with other internal sensations such as breathing. Look in the mirror and notice the changes that are occurring in your posture. Notice your posture, face and jaw adjust and your eyes become brighter. Notice, perhaps, that you have a wider angle in your field of view versus a narrowly focused one. Notice your Zone FEEL start to blossom as the NO-Zone FEEL fades.

3) Shift in this manner, from the Zone experience to the NO-Zone experience, three or four times. Notice how easy it is to shift into the Zone, and, conversely, to fall out of it. You now know how to do it. You now know how it feels — GPS. Equipped with your own GPS, you will never have an excuse to be out of the Zone again.

What you think about (or what others get you to think about) affects your Zone and predicts how you will play. The mirror tells the story, except that you now have a set of internal sensations that allow you to identify and guide yourself into the Zone. Learn them and use them.

Chapter Summary

Get used to the guidance of your Zone FEEL and your NO-Zone FEEL. Get used to shifting away from the NO Zone every time you feel it creeping in. Perhaps write down what pulls you out — simply out of curiosity. Become aware of how your body is a natural bio-feedback device, where your Zone FEEL and NO-Zone FEEL are as useful as traffic lights.

As you progress in the SportExcel System, you will need your signals right out there in plain sight (or plain feeling), so that you can stop looking for success in the rearview mirror. In the next chapter, I will illustrate the type of GPS you can get from self-talk — a very obvious symptom of too much thinking.

11 Self-talk Blues

Self-talk — positive or negative — will derail your game faster than orange targets on an orange background.

*"I never looked at the consequences of missing a big shot...
when you think about the consequences you always think of a
negative result."*

— Michael Jordan, Star Basketball Player

As a high-performance coach and trainer I have worked with hundreds of very talented athletes, many of whom who had lost the passion in their sports for any number of reasons. Some are related to past performance, some are related to problems with learning and others are related to athletic self-perception. However, my findings indicate that the number one reason for losing passion is due to a history of having an overbearing, obnoxious or abusive person involved in their athletic life — coach, athlete, parent or competitor. And the number two reason is due to the athlete's continuing to relive the negative effects of this person — long, long after — by way of "self-talk."

Self-talk GPS is Learned Behavior

Self-talk is a substantial part of our GPS guidance system. It is our masterful ability to say nice and un-nice things to ourselves in life generally, and in competitive situations specifically. "Remember to be strong and confident" is a positive one. It sounds nice, but if your opponent said it you'd be distracted and a bit irritated. And then there is the negative, "You stupid idiot, how could you do a dumb thing like that," the effect of which is self-explanatory.

The difficulty with self-talk is that, although we might be guarded (and sometimes follow) the positive and negative advice we hear from other competitors, when we say the same comments to ourselves they go right into our psyche — unguarded, unquestioned, and unevaluated. Because of this, self-talk is very destructive as it is like having no firewall on your computer to protect against internet hacking and viruses.

Self-talk tells you that some underlying NO-Zone experience has just surfaced. Listen to athletes when the bottom falls out of their game. They give themselves all sorts of advice, most of which is less than flattering. "You've hit this blinking shot a million times. How could you be so careless?" It is abusive to both them and the rest of us who have to listen to it.

On the other hand, athletes who are in the Zone have NO self-talk. They might use a few words here and there to guide themselves via self-coaching, but they are usually in the present moment and have no need to listen to positive or negative comments from themselves or others. They just play, and it feels good — 'Zone FEEL' kind of good.

How Self-talk Gets Started

I had the opportunity to travel to Georgia to work with Coach Mike Simpson and his team of young athletes who were preparing for the U.S. Junior Olympics. Mike Simpson is an international clay target coach whose dedication has had him honored in Georgia State's Assembly as the Volunteer of the Year. He's the kind of coach who forgoes vacations in order to build a facility to keep his world-class athletes in training. I admire Coach Mike's work. He has a powerful bearing and a voice that is empowering — he uses a kind word with one athlete who might be struggling, and a corrective suggestion to another to keep her in the Zone.

Mike has some amazing stories, and during the course of the weekend he told me about a young athlete he had taken to a national competition a few years ago. At the event, the young athlete had had an extraordinary day, and, when they got back to the hotel, where the rest of the athletes were excitedly preparing to call and brag to their parents, this young man told Coach Mike and his teammates that he hoped his dad would *not* call. Ultimately, however, a call from the dad came through.

The young man enthusiastically described his successful day to the dad, but at the end of the call he hung up the phone and fell silent. When Coach Mike asked what happened, the boy reported what his father had said to him: "That's great, but you'll only screw up tomorrow." The next day the father's prediction came true as the young man's game did fall apart. Was the father able to see into the future, or, as we might suspect, did he have a role in the making of it, planting the seeds of the boy's own self-talk?

Another example of the destructive power of self-talk relates to my friend Gordon (not his real name). We played sports together a few years ago and he could be very hard on himself. With nearly every mistake, rather than taking it as guidance and fixing the problem, he beat himself up and cussed up a storm. On one occasion I had had enough of his outbursts and asked him if he would ever speak to his son like that. He looked at me curiously and said no, and I immediately replied, "Then why do you speak to yourself that way?" He stopped, thought for just a brief moment and then started swearing at me, telling me to mind my own [expletive deleted] business. I had a good laugh (to myself) because my comment stopped Gordon's verbal self-abuse — at least out loud.

Self-talk has to start somewhere, and I believe that we learn to talk to ourselves in the same manner others talk to us. That young athlete's dad and Coach Mike are going to greatly influence this young man's thinking (and self-talk) for the rest of his life. The message of intolerance for mistakes and failure from his dad are going to be the flip side of the message of understanding and empowerment from Coach Mike. Who this young man chooses to model will result in whether he ends up talking to himself like my friend Gordon, his dad or Coach Mike.

Fixing Self-talk

Why should you fix self-talk? Because it reveals obvious NO-Zone experiences from your past that can be fixed. If you avoid fixing the problem, the self-talk will keep right on doing more damage. Our subconscious minds are very child-like. They take things literally; everything is personal. Self-comments such as "I'm clumsy" or "I'm stupid" or "I'm incompetent" go directly to our subconscious minds and affect us deeply. When you have been talked to in this way as a child, it is very easy for you to continue to abuse yourself, without ever being aware of it. I call it the *self-talk blues*. This is completely unnecessary and, fortunately, easy to change. We just have to catch ourselves doing it — and that can be the hard part.

Spend some time with any group of athletes and you'll hear all manner of outbursts. Some of us curse at ourselves. Some of us complain and whine about our incompetence. Some of us threaten ourselves with bodily injury and death. Some of us belittle and mock ourselves. And how do our bodies react? With hangdog posture, weakness, erratic breathing and worse. Yes worse, because we sometimes believe that *others* expect us to display atonement like this after a failure. It can be a big act for their benefit. And I don't know about you, but I'd rather empower myself to smile and get excited by the possibilities of recovering from the mistake.

To stop this kind of behavior, all you have to do is ask yourself: "Would I talk to another person like this — a child learning to walk, a friend learning to golf, a spouse learning to play the piano?" If you answered no, then fix it. The good news is that you can correct this kind of self-behavior by being a "Coach Mike" type of mentor for yourself when you identify it. Start by shifting to your Zone FEEL and it will probably turn most of it off entirely.

The even better news is that simply by using it as guidance you can get some pretty terrific results fairly quickly. For those of us who are older athletes, it may take more time, but get used to understanding it as GPS and simply apply the tools you will learn in the rest of this book to resolve it. The pay-off is that, aside from our own improved performance, there are tremendous benefits for those around you, whether you are a coach of impressionable young athletes or a parent, teammate, friend, corporate leader or grandparent.

Exercise: Curing the Self-talk Blues

1) Understand that self-talk is GPS. In a simple reworking of the GOLDEN RULE, "Treat yourself like you would want others to treat you." It starts with you. Identify your Zone FEEL and get into it at the outset of any competition and maintain it.

2) When you lose the Zone, listen to how you talk to yourself. Here are some self-talk examples you might catch yourself saying: "Don't screw it up." "Those mistakes kill me." "I certainly didn't come to play." "Boy did I suck." "The guys on this team really pull me down."

3) Shift back to your Zone FEEL if you can and notice how quiet your brain gets. In the following chapters there will be lots of strategies to help you with this.

One myth in common practice is that we need to displace negative self-talk with positive self-talk or affirmations such as, "I am powerful" or "I am focused" or "I am worthy." The notion is that the more frequently you whisper affirmations of this sort in your head, the sooner they'll become positive, permanent and continuing motivational messages. Quite simply, affirmations require thinking. I suggest, instead, that you use self-talk, once identified, as merely a NO-Zone indicator and fix it.

Chapter Summary

You now know how you want to be coached, or parented, or talked to. So, do unto yourself as you would have others do unto you. Keep yourself on the pathway to the Zone by being the best coach to yourself that you can be — a Mike Simpson type of coach. Identify your Zone FEEL, identify your NO-Zone FEEL, and be supportive of yourself as you learn to fix what the self-talk is telling you. In the next chapter, we'll look at a whole range of self-talk type issues that we will now refer to as blocks (to performance).

12 Don't Think of Your Big Toe

Mental blocks — making mole hills into mountains.

"When anyone tells me I can't do anything...
I'm just not listening anymore."

— Florence Griffith-Joyner, Star Track Athlete

One summer I walked the golf course with one of my clients and had him practice the skills he had learned with which to stay in the Zone. The golf course was beautiful, the man's game was focused, the weather was exceptional and then it started to turn ugly. Not the weather — me. I started talking non-stop, crinkled a water bottle and told a very a good joke (that he didn't get.) I warned him it was coming, and he listened — to everything.

I was testing his ability to stay in the Zone by setting blocks in the way of his game. Oh yes, he knew his outcome was to stay in the Zone and to play well, but I had my outcome as well, and that was to teach him a lesson. My outcome was to get him to accept my devious task of undermining his game. And I was having fun planting suggestions for him to plunk his ball in the water hazard, or slice it into the rough, or skip it across the green into the sand.

And I must have been very good at it, because he accepted my outcomes very quickly. His first shot did plunk into the water hazard; the second shot lay slightly in the rough; the third was way short of the green; the fourth was a long putt to the hole; and the fifth a two-putt. In summary, I had effectively drawn his attention away from HIS outcome to birdie the hole to my outcome for him of wrecking his game. I set up some very effective blocks to his success.

The Level of Inattention Triggers GPS

Our level of attention (or inattention) is the product of how powerful our outcomes are. You now know that it is better for us to set deliberate, powerful outcomes rather than let them be set inadvertently by subconscious minds or by others. However, outcomes do get misdirected and we need to identify when that happens, because these types of blocks trigger our GPS, even when delivered "out of our awareness" at a subconscious level. Crinkling water bottles, we can challenge; subliminal suggestions from advertisers or hints to make mistakes, we can't. People — some devious, some inadvertent — can dredge up and trigger past No-Zone experiences of failure and we are letting them.

Big Toe Suggestions

In my workshops I demonstrate how distractions work by giving several directives in a row: Don't think of your big toe. Don't listen to the noises outside of the room. Don't notice your breathing. Don't feel your shirt against the skin on your back. With each directive it is clear that the participants are changing their attention according to the directive. Were they attempting to play their game, their minds would be all over the place and I'd be a very successful block to their success. In the workshop setting, it drives participants crazy, and they seem powerless to stop me, at least until they identify what I'm doing — by GPS. When they do, that's the time for them to shift gears.

Distracting comments come in all shapes and sizes, both in practice or competition. I'm sure you have heard many of them, and golfers offer up some of the best: "Your swing looks good; what have you changed?" "The first hole is always the most difficult." "How is the change in your stance coming along?" "Does your arm still hurt?" "Sure is windy." "Man, the trees make the fairways tight."

Each statement does a remarkable job of drawing your attention away from parring the hole. Hence, one of the most important rules in any sport is that you get what you think about (or what others want you to think about). Therefore, you must ensure that you control this process in yourself or in the athletes you coach.

Coach Greevy's Test

Olympic Development Coach Les Greevy created an exercise where he deliberately put his athletes through a lengthy, rigorous workout and then gave them a simulated competition. They were exhausted and did poorly. He could have ended the practice and said: "Hey, you guys have had it, let's call it a day." But that would simply have drawn their attention to the block that says: "When I'm tired I perform poorly." Instead, he gave them five minutes to rest and told them to think about their best competition ever. Just by this subtle change in attention, they did considerably better. He had drawn their attention to their resources of perseverance, skill and determination. And this is precisely what you'll start doing with the tools you'll learn in the next section, Step 4 of the SportExcel System.

By now you have the prerequisite GPS system in place to identify how blocks such as the weather, obnoxious people or fatigue affect you — and you may already be using your Zone and No-Zone FEEL signals to routinely assist in understanding and resolving them up. (If not, go back to Chapters 2 and 3 and learn the signals.) With this GPS skill, you control the process and know instantly that you've gone off the rails, have a block to fix or, more specifically, have to challenge a specific person's comments.

And what is even more exciting here is that when you consciously and repeatedly identify your blocks, your brain learns how to do it subconsciously and then automatically activates the tools to fix the blocks. You will learn powerful tools in the following chapters so that you (and your brain) can understand and resolve almost every imaginable block to your game. Your consistency, winning and success depend on it.

Chapter Summary

Throughout all your practice and competition, you are beginning to learn to identify blocks that pull your attention away from your game. The golfer I mentioned at the outset lost attentiveness when I crinkled a water bottle. Coach Greevy's young athletes, on the other hand, stayed attentive even when tired. By identifying and removing your blocks, you too will learn to think of Zone FEEL, instead of "your big toe." So, without further ado, as I've already mentioned the powerful tools offered in Step 4 of the SportExcel System, let's get started fixing your blocks.

Get comfortable with your ability to identify a wide range of GPS guidance before moving on.

Step 4

Tools for Success

Trying to be positive, grounded and present
causes us to think.
We need tools to help us __not__ think.

"What I hear, I forget. What I see, I remember.
What I do, I understand."

— **Confucius, Star Philosopher**

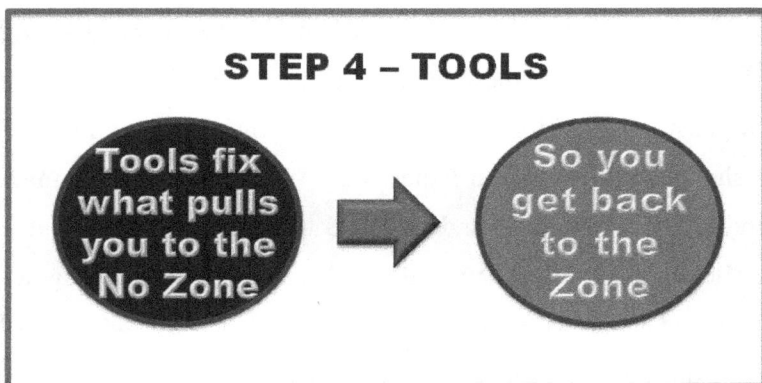

STEP 4 – TOOLS

Tools fix what pulls you to the No Zone ⇒ So you get back to the Zone

13 Block Busters: Getting Back on Track

Learning a new behavior takes 28 days
of repetitive behavior — NOT.

"The difference is almost all mental. The top players just hate to lose.
I think that's the difference. A champion hates to lose
even more than she loves to win."

— Chris Evert, Star Tennis Player

Example 1

On my way to present a workshop in Texas, I was listening to a radio call-in show where a woman described her experience with a ghost. She said she was driving uneventfully along the highway when she heard her deceased father yell, "Watch out!" She slammed on the brakes and swerved — and managed to avoid a boulder right in her path. Clearly the woman viewed this as her father's spirit saving her life. However, I view it as an awareness strategy that made full use of her subconscious mind to help her react to adversity.

Example 2

I was conducting a workshop in Northern Ontario. A participant related a story about how he was piloting his bush plane and the engine quit in mid-flight. Pilots are trained to go through a checklist to restart the aircraft, but what surprised him was that he was doing it from "outside" the aircraft, looking back at himself and giving advice in a very calm, dispassionate voice. He said he matter-of-factly followed the advice and restarted the engine. He felt it was bizarre and had never told anyone about it. I told him it was simply a subconscious strategy that I teach in advanced workshops to help athletes step back and gain perspective.

Example 3

A banker friend of mine told me a story of how he successfully shut down a small bank because employees were defrauding the customers of millions of dollars. He described interviewing the manager and the board members, and reading over the accounting books. He told me he had felt uneasy, but there was nothing obvious he could put his finger on. Nonetheless, he called in forensic auditors and they discovered that several million dollars in inappropriate loans had been made. I told him it was one of the best uses of a strategy — albeit subconscious — ever described to me.

Example 4

A young golfer I was working with had a wildly inconsistent drive off the tee. His father laughed and told me that his son could mimic the drives of 10 or so professional golfers and it was very impressive to watch. I told him that his son's mimicking skill would make him great or be his worst nightmare, as he was using his subconscious ability to copy others.

Example 5

An Olympic Skeet shooter told me he could slow the target down, make it appear as large as a garbage-can lid and make it turn bright orange at the moment he need to pull the trigger. I told him that this was an incredible strategy that others would pay huge money to have.

Nothing New Under the Sun

What unifies and connects these examples is the very powerful and effective tools that each of these people used in times of need or crisis. They were subconscious tools — no thinking required. We all have these kinds of tools, whether we are aware of them or not. We use them to create excellence at work or in our sport, maintain our sanity and enhance our ability to connect with others. Sometimes we apply them inadequately, after the fact or only under duress, but we do apply them.

Think about it. How many times have we heard the following?

"Just breathe between shifts."

"Go for a walk and let off some steam."

"Relax."

"Count to 10."

"Step back from this and get some perspective.

"How do you think (insert any name) would handle that?"

"Perform in the game like you do in practice."

"It is just the fairway and you, nobody else."

Many of these hints or suggestions seem too simple to be useful as tools in our game as we hear them expressed day in and day out. Up until this moment, you might not even have thought of them as tools, and especially not as elite, high-performance tools. But they are, especially when we can learn simple ways to access them on demand and create a huge impact on our game.

The point I'm making here is that the tools you are about to learn in *Step 4* of the *SportExcel System* are simply what every elite athlete you have ever seen already knows how to use. And soon, so will you. They'll be presented in an easy-to-understand format, so that you, the novice athlete can use them subconsciously (just like you do any new technique in your game) to bust through your mental blocks, and you, the elite athlete, can understand the tools you already use and apply them even better and sooner. You will learn each tool in a step-by-step process and apply them consciously at first. But very soon, with practice, these new tools will operate efficiently at the subconscious level, in the very same way they operate for pros and Olympians. So, follow the instructions, work them diligently and be patient — but not too patient.

New Ways to Think of Change

With the tools that follow, each and every one of you will learn new ways to break old habits, learn new skills and gain perspective. You will learn what it means to step back and look at problems differently. You will learn how to step into the shoes of your sporting heroes and model any specific skill. You'll learn to step back from a problematic relationship and fix what is bothering you regardless of frustration, anger or irritant. You'll learn to slow down the game and make any venue feel like it is your favorite. And, with a bit of practice, you'll have all the tools working for you subconsciously, just like the individuals who were mentioned in the opening examples.

Stories of the Tools in Action

As well, you'll be presented with short stories accompanying each tool, describing how various athletes, coaches, parents and sports leaders have used the tools of the system. Of course, their names are omitted to ensure confidentiality, but I can assure you that the stories are true and truly representative of how you too will have the opportunity to make similar, amazing changes in your game. They may also give you some creative ideas as to how to use the various tools.

Chapter Summary

You now know how to identify your Zone FEEL and NO-Zone FEEL. You know how to set and enhance your goals so that they drive you toward success and winning. You know the importance of identifying problems with your game as simply GPS — important evidence that will help you to make corrections and move on to the next level. Now be prepared to learn the tools of Step 4 of the SportExcel System — starting with learning to forget.

14 Learning to Forget

School teaches us to remember the good,

the bad and the ugly.

Now you're gonna learn to forget.

"I never learned anything from a match that I won."

— Bobby Jones, Star Golfer

As a young hockey player I'd often come off the ice after a shift and have one of my teammates comment about a great play or a mistake our line had made. I'd listen and wonder how I had missed it. Was I in the same game? And if it had happened, shouldn't I have remembered it as well? I remember wondering if I was losing it.

This 'forgetting' I had experienced is explained in an article by Dr. Bob Rotella, entitled, *"How to Drain 'em Like Jack,"* in Golf Digest (June 2001). The story goes something like this: While speaking with the public, Jack Nicklaus made the claim that he had never three-putted or missed a putt from inside five feet on the last hole of a tournament. A spectator stood up at the end of the talk and informed Mr. Nicklaus that his statement was incorrect and that he had actually seen Jack miss a three-foot putt on the last hole of a Senior PGA event. Jack respectfully denied it, but the man persisted and even offered to send a videotape of the putt. Jack told the man that there was no need to send anything, because he had been there.

When Jack left the meeting, the man persisted and asked why Jack couldn't admit to making a mistake. Rotella, the moderator, asked the man if he played golf. "Yes." Did he have a handicap? "Yes, 16." And, if he missed a putt on the last hole of an important tournament, would he remember it? "Of course I would." Rotella's reply was this: "So let me get this straight. You're a 16-handicap, and Jack Nicklaus is the greatest golfer ever, and you want Jack to think like you?" The man had no answer.

The point of course is that elite athletes only remember what helps them, whereas the average athlete remembers everything. In the early part of Nicklaus' career, forgetting may not have been as easy. He probably felt just as sick about his mistakes as you do. He may even have recycled mistakes over and over in his mind. But he knew what he wanted and he was persistent. It may have taken hours of practice initially, but to become great he eventually got it right. And over his career, erasing memories became easier and easier until, ultimately, his memory became subconsciously selective.

Forgetting Happens Naturally — Why Wait?

Our minds often forget bad experiences over time, simply by the addition and sheer volume of other experiences that are more pleasant. Some memories are resistant to this, but, by and large, memories fade or get edged out over time. But why wait for the pleasant memory to crowd out the unpleasant? Why wait for the empowering experiences to crowd out the disempowering? Why wait for happy experiences to crowd out the sad? Let's learn to do it now by using our natural ability to mix and jumble memories together in very positive ways.

In the early part of the 20th Century, Russian physiologist Ivan Pavlov performed an experiment where he rang a bell each time he gave dogs their dinner. Before long, the dogs associated the sound of the bell with food, in the same way the typical house pet comes running to the sound of the kibble bag being opened. Simply by ringing the bell, Pavlov could get the dogs salivating for food. The sound of the bell was attached in the dog's memory to food. This is called an anchor — an auditory anchor — because it is directly attached (anchored) to the memory called food — just as a boat is attached to the lake bottom by the real thing, the boat anchor.

As humans, we exhibit the same response to anchors, just as Pavlov's dogs did, and it is an important part of how we learn to avoid being burned by a stove element on the second encounter. Our anchors are many — sight, sound and touch. When a person passes by and waves at us, we feel pleasant (hey, that person is nice). Even if the person is a stranger, the wave is usually anchored to happy memories and we respond favorably. On the other hand, when a person passes by and gives us a scowl and holds up his middle finger, we have another instantaneous response, probably less than pleasant (hey, what is his problem?) as that finger gesture is usually attached to negative responses. (I once demonstrated this in a workshop and lost the favor of the participants for a good 30 minutes and have never done it again.) Just like Pavlov's bell produced instant salivation in the dogs, anchors such as these gestures are linked to our human subconscious responses — instant smiling or instant fuming.

Anchors Away

Anchors attach themselves to all situations. In sports, great feelings are attached to the light, perfect feel of sporting equipment, the crisp, bright image of a goal being scored, the warmth and excitement of cheering fans, the solidness of a perfect stance, the smoothness of a runner's pace and the sweet spot as a bat connects with a baseball. And bad feelings can become attached to gut-sinking mistakes, distracting comments, awkward miscues, destabilizing gusts of wind and obnoxious gestures. The actual response to these anchors can be smiles and adrenalized excitement or curses and tantrums — all of which are triggered automatically — by accidental and purposeful gestures, comments and touches.

But there's good news. We can redirect how we respond to these kinds of anchors. Because of our brain's subconscious ability to be aware of several things at once, we can actually use the anchoring process to help us forget NO-Zone experiences. We can, for example, take any NO-Zone *moment of disaster* where you remember feeling awful — the game was an embarrassment, the coach singled you out, a mistake lost you the game, or the game was lost after a "sure" victory — and mix it with Zone *moments of brilliance* when your game felt wonderful — you won a championship, made a tryout, or clawed your way out of a big hole to win. And, just like two different types of metal can make an even stronger alloy when combined, the memories of your NO-Zone and Zone experiences will be permanently and positively fused.

The following exercise allows you to do this. You'll be creating an anchor to capture a NO-Zone experience, such as Jack Nicklaus' miss from under five feet. And then you'll be creating an anchor to capture a number of powerful Zone experiences, such as the many times Jack won the U.S. Open. And, rather than let the passage of time do the work for you, you'll fuse these two memories together. In the blink of an eye, you'll learn to forget and get back to winning — just like Jack.

Exercise: FUSING

1) Take a moment to remember a competition-related, NO-Zone experience that felt terrible. See it, feel it, hear it. Not pleasant is it? Pinch your LEFT thumb and index finger together. It is the anchor that captures the NO-Zone memory in the very same way Pavlov's bell captured the salivating hunger of the dogs. Release your fingers after a few moments.

2) Now think of a Zone experience where you were relaxed and wired and where you could perform without thinking. Relive the memory fully and experience the wonderful Zone FEEL. With your RIGHT hand this time, pinch your thumb and index finger together to capture the Zone memory. This is your Zone Anchor. You now have two opposing anchors, but let's not take chances

here. Repeat step two and capture (pinch with your right hand) two more powerful Zone experiences — the stronger the better. Go for it and ensure they have an over-the-top sense of power!

3) Now you get to have some fun. Pinch both your left NO-Zone anchor and your right Zone Anchor *at the same time*. There may be initial confusion, but the shift is usually immediate and after a few minutes you'll find it very difficult — if not impossible — to get back to the NO-Zone memory.

Scarred for Life? Not

It is now within your power and skillset to resolve almost any memory that pulls you out of the Zone — weather, crowds, obnoxious teammates, nervousness, etc. When you make a mistake and feel bad, FUSE Zone experiences to that NO-Zone. Frustrated with a teammate? FUSE Zone experiences to that NO-Zone. Feel your posture slouching and going into the "hang dog" routine? FUSE Zone experiences so that you straighten your posture up. And if it doesn't work the first time, repeat it until it does. The more often you FUSE memories, the quicker and more proficient you will get at forgetting the bad and the ugly, just like Jack, so that the process of forgetting negative experiences becomes an automatic, subconscious habit.

Chapter Summary

As a young athlete I had it right about forgetting the past and staying in the moment. Your ability to fix and forget bad memories, instead of letting them accumulate and cause a downward spiral of mistakes, puts you on the road to owning your game. When someone says, "Watch out for the wind today" and it reminds you of your worst, windy-day score ever, you'll know how to fuse the memory — so it never returns. In the next chapter, I'll give you further examples of why learning to forget is so important.

FUSING in Action: Hockey

❝ Bob was invited to one of my tryouts where he noticed that I was a bit hesitant whenever I had the puck on my stick. I told him that in hockey you barely ever touch the puck. Over a career it might be only a total of six minutes! I also told him that everyone watches you when you have the puck and it can be stressful. Bob didn't buy this explanation and told me that everyone watched me body check opposing players too, and that I seemed to love that. I smiled, as it really teaches my opponents to keep their heads up.

So Bob had me anchor memories of my best body checks and FUSE them to memories of me carrying the puck. Hesitancy immediately disappeared, forgotten. The confidence I now feel is unbelievable, and I've been known to do a few spectacular end-to-end rushes. From here on in, I expect that the remainder of my "six minutes" will be exceptional. **❞**

— Hockey Player

15 Love to Make Mistakes

The irony is that the better you feel after making a mistake, the fewer mistakes you'll make.

"Every strike brings me closer to the next home run."

— *Babe Ruth, Star Baseball Player*

There is a sad fact about training in any sport and it is this: The more you strive to get to the next level, the more mistakes you'll make. And the more mistakes you make, the more it can hurt to make mistakes (even as you might be becoming a better athlete.) Similarly, the more tournaments or competitions you enter, the more you'll have the opportunity to make even more mistakes, at least at the outset. And the more people you meet at these tournaments or competitions, the greater the likelihood that you'll be embarrassed many more times by those mistakes than if you had just stayed at home and watched a movie.

Glass Half Empty

I know I'm looking at your game from the perspective of a glass half empty versus one half full, but go to any competition and a huge number of coaches and athletes get very upset by mistakes — theirs and the officials. So I'm figuring that they must have practiced making mistakes (a lot) to get that annoyed with them or embarrassed by them. So there must be a "glass half empty" group that needs help. Even though they know that learning from mistakes is part of improving their game, accumulated mistakes are taking a toll on many of them.

So it bears asking the question: Why do we do this to ourselves? Is it the hope of riches and fame? For some, but not for many in sport. So what is it then? Is it the challenge? Maybe, but with the behaviors I've seen across many sports, a lot of athletes would like it to be a lot simpler. Is it the friendship? That is a given, but many athletes might want to read the book: "*How to Win Friends and Influence People*," by Dale Carnegie. Is it the level of machismo? Perhaps. And even a willingness to be cannon fodder so that others may bask in their glory of victory at your expense.

So besides being great physical exercise and sometimes providing lots of fresh air and sun (depending on the sport), I'm stumped as to why so many would willingly practice making mistake after mistake and:

1) Be nervous at the future prospect of making them;

2) Get angry at actually making them;

    AND

3) Be distracted by others making them.

Enjoying Adversity

I apologize for sounding negative here, but the emotional angst caused by mistakes is serious and there is a better way. I stumbled upon it during my competitive karate career:

You have to enjoy adversity (love to make mistakes)
before you can ever enjoy winning.

In my case with the martial arts, I had to "enjoy" the mistake of failing to block an attack (and the pain of getting hurt), whether from my own lack of skill or someone else's over-exuberance.

Allow me to explain. In the sport of point karate, all combatants are supposed to exercise incredible control, and techniques (punches and kicks) are supposed to be stopped, just before full contact is made. In a wild and furious sparring match, control often gets lost and combatants may inadvertently inflict pain upon each other. So, in order to do well at sparring, I had to accept the inevitable pain as I built up my experience. Every bit of pain had to be a motivator — a powerful motivator — to get better and stronger and faster so that I could get more skillful at avoiding pain — or inflicting it on others. I had to love every hurt, as only then would it lift me higher and higher into the Zone. Once again, this is fabulous in theory.

So I tested a simple mantra: "I love sparring." This little phrase served as something other than an affirmation. It immediately ignited that good feeling of my Zone, something I had rarely experienced at the time, and resulted in a relaxed feeling I'd never felt before in sparring. And once

I got used to that feeling, the following weeks and months of training produced huge gains in confidence and fun. It was not pain-free, although it must have helped by producing endorphins to get me through it, as pain usually surfaced on the drive home from the practice or competition.

Exercise: Enjoy the Pain

In most sports there is emotional pain from making mistakes. This exercise will help you to enjoy that pain:

1) Remember a rather emotionally painful game or competition and watch it in your mind's eye, from start to finish. You'll be surprised at the kind of detail you'll remember. Notice specifically where you went off track — beginning, middle or end of the game or competition. Pinch your left fingers (FUSING) at that precise moment of a mistake and anchor the NO-Zone feeling — frustration, anger, embarrassment, pain — via the first step of the FUSING exercise you learned in the previous chapter.

2) Pinch your right fingers as you accumulate three successive Zone experiences where you felt powerful and in the Zone.

3) Pinch both hand pinches simultaneously.

4) Continue to review your "tape" and clean up all mistakes from that game experience.

And that is it. You can now replay your memory of your past experience and notice that the "pain" of losing is most likely gone. Vanished. Continue in this manner with any other painful or embarrassing events, and past mistakes will start to feel good.

The pain of mistakes must never be carried over to the next part of your game or a future competition. By learning this approach to resolving mistakes, you'll likely prevent a second mistake from happening, period. And, with practice, you'll be teaching your subconscious mind to resolve mistakes instantly, so that the death spiral, where your game goes out of control, will be a thing of the past.

FUSING in Action: Track

" The nice thing about international competitions is that they are usually telecast and my friends and family get to see them. Bob told me that he could use the same videos to analyze my events, but I must say that I was skeptical. And when he was able to tell me exactly the four or five places in my 800 meter run where I had lost valuable seconds, I was convinced. He said he was able to do it by watching changes in my Zone, but that doesn't matter here. What does matter is that he had me re-run the race in my mind, and I felt myself losing the Zone at each spot. At one point in the race, for example, I lost it when a runner passed me. At another, I lost it when I saw that my split time was slower than I wanted. And similarly, I lost it in the last 75 meters of the races.

Bob had me anchor each of those spots and FUSE them to Zone experiences. And, at the next event, I stayed strong throughout the whole race, even when runners made a move to pass me at various times, probably just trying to intimidate me. I stayed in my Zone, stuck to my plan, and overtook them exactly where I needed to. **"**

— Track Athlete

Chapter Summary

Learn to "love" the mistakes and your pre-game fears will evaporate. Once the mistake has absolutely no effect on you, you'll relax and be able to focus on what you have to do now, every time, from start to finish. And make sure after every competition to fix your mistakes. The FUSING exercise works wonderfully here, as you get to copy your past brilliance. If, on the other hand, you have had too few moments of brilliance, in the next chapter you'll learn how to fix and resolve weak parts of your game by copying the brilliance of professionals, Olympians and other fantastic athletes.

16 Learning New Skills is Child's Play

As a kid I became my hockey hero, played like him and won like him.

"The best and fastest way to learn a sport is to watch and imitate a champion."

— Jean-Claude Killy, Star Skier

I have had the opportunity to work with many coaches, athletes, business people, professionals and a mix of professional singers, dancers and musicians from around the world. A common theme, if any, has been that of failure or defeat and the intense emotional content it carries. The FUSING tool you just learned works well to resolve any type of disappointment because you already have many experiences of success. It is a very flexible technique that allows you to customize it to specific situations. Your body is a vast encyclopedia of knowledge for this purpose — visual acuity, technique, strength and power — except when you are faced with something completely new and strange and you draw a blank.

What if, in your sport career, you have only played at an amateur level and you get the opportunity to take your game to the professional level, where the game is faster and is played by bigger opponents? What if you are a specialist in one position and are asked to take on a new role? What if you are new at a sport such as triathlon and have one very weak discipline?

Many times we face situations like these that require a whole new level of skills. We get frustrated when we try to adapt existing skills — FUSING — with limited success. As human beings, though, we have an incredible ability to learn by watching others. And as adults, it may simply be a matter of reawakening the learning tools we once took for granted.

The Blank Slate Gets Filled Up

As kids, we were pretty much a blank slate skill-wise and so we learned quickly. Any frustration was rare or brief. We have no conscious recollection of how we learned; we watched adults and older siblings throw a ball or jump a fence and somehow we just knew how to do it as well. We watched our sports heroes, parents and mentors compete and we somehow learned the presence and poise of competing as well. We watched and in the process learned to talk, walk, catch or hit a small white ball traveling at great speed.

But many of us as competitive athletes now find the ease of learning new skills to be more elusive. Perhaps because of pressure, big expectations, self-consciousness or fear, we begin to anticipate failure and forget how to learn. As a child I played masterful hockey on the pond but when it came to the organized rink — poof — my skill was gone, as if in a cloud of smoke. As teenagers or adults, somehow we need to bypass our fears, doubts and frustrations and get back to an ability to learn and be undeterred by failure. We simply need to see it done and then do it ourselves. Or, do it again and again and again until we succeed, like a child bound and determined to walk, just like his parents.

The Modeling Process

As a young golfer, I remember going out to the golf course for the first time with my friends and, with rented clubs, shooting par for the course. I look back on that now and muse that it was impossible. But then again, I *didn't know* it was impossible at the time. I was just having fun playing and probably pretending I was Arnold Palmer, my namesake. More importantly, the only place I'd seen anyone golfing was on TV, and they were the best in the world. I realize now that I was doing one heck of a job copying the Arnold Palmers of the world.

Today, what I did no longer surprises me, as I remember displaying similar feats in hockey, badminton and any other sports. I saw an athlete, stepped into his shoes and became him. The way I learned — the way we all learn — is through a process in the brain that science calls mirror neurons (*The Mirror-Neuron System*, Giacomo Rizzolatti and Laila Craighero, Annual Review Neuroscience, 2004. 27:169–92). It is our natural learning process. As adults, perhaps due to fears, doubts and frustrations, we sometimes block our ability to learn and often consider learning new skills to be the reserve of the young. Fortunately, you can resurrect your natural ability at any age. And, with an exercise called TALENT MODE (a play on the title of *The Talent Code*, with due respect paid to author Daniel Coyle), you'll be able to learn any skill in the same way you learned how to walk, talk and catch a ball, as long as you've seen someone else doing it.

Exercise: TALENT MODE

1) Think of a skill that you would like to improve. It can involve any situation where you consistently have a No-Zone FEEL, make mistakes, lose your focus or just want to be faster, stronger and smarter.

2) Now imagine yourself in the bleachers overlooking your venue. Imagine all the delightful sights, feelings and sounds of the event.

3) Looking down upon the venue to the RIGHT, imagine someone playing the game. That person, who looks and sounds like you, displays the shaky skill you wish to improve — he or she is clearly demonstrating incompetence.

4) Look to your immediate LEFT. Imagine three elite athletes (who have the skills you would like to learn) stepping up beside you. These athletes display the skillful excellence of their game, similar to what Arnold Palmer displayed for me. You may see them in living color, black and white, or just know they are there, as each of us imagines our images uniquely.

5) Physically step to your LEFT and imagine stepping into the shoes of the first elite athlete. Notice any sensations and changes in your posture as you do this. Wait a few seconds and then step LEFT into the shoes of the second elite athlete. Finally, step LEFT into the shoes of the third elite athlete.

6) After a few seconds, look back out to the venue to your RIGHT and invite the person who looks like you to come back over "inside you", in order to teach that YOU what you learned from stepping into the shoes of the elite athletes.

7) Now imagine a future practice or competition where your new skill would come into play. Play it through in your mind and check for the Zone FEEL. If it's there in abundance, go out and test the new skill in your game. If it is not present, redo the exercise until you can feel it. Remember that you learned this way as a child and, if it seems too easy, when was learning to walk or talk ever difficult for you then?

Applying TALENT MODE to Everything

Starting today, I want you to watch athletes at competitive levels higher than you, in person, on TV or on YouTube. Absorb what they do without looking for specific technique. After each viewing, use TALENT MODE and notice how you feel. As well, use TALENT MODE during breaks in your training. In this case, you can simply imagine yourself stepping sideways (to avoid stepping on any toes.) Be prepared for an accelerated learning curve — especially when you apply it in every area of your sport and life.

Chapter Summary

Thus far in the book, you have had the opportunity to learn several definitive skills. You now have the means to acquire the Zone with your Zone FEEL and NO-Zone FEEL signals — Step 1 of the SportExcel System. You have a way to make your dreams of winning come to life with DÉJÀ-VU DVD in Step 2. You know that everything that happens to you — the good, the bad and the ugly — can be utilized in terms of GPS, which is Step 3.   And now, along with FUSING, you have TALENT MODE so that you can model both yourself and anyone else in any area of your life — Step 4. This is just the beginning. It is a simple tool kit. Take it with you to your game and practice it, before you move on. And then, in the next chapter, I'll get you walking so powerfully that no competitor will ever bother you again.

TALENT MODE in Action: Collegiate Football

" One of the hardest things an athlete can do is to go for a tryout. You have so much riding on making the team, especially for a college team that you've been dreaming of playing for. And it doesn't matter how many people tell you that you are good or that you can make it or to just relax and take it one drill at a time. Panic sets in and you don't hear it. You just want it over with.

One of my weaknesses was the 40-yard dash and it is so crucial to have a good time, especially for a linebacker position. Bob took me through TALENT MODE and I was able to step into the shoes of several NFLers. After that, it felt wholly different — fast and powerful. I made the team and saw some great playing time in my freshman season, and even made the second team all-star team that year. **"**

— Football Player

17 Posture is Everything

As a kid I slouched, not realizing that posture was both a window to my soul and the means of recovering it.

"All battles are won before they are fought."

— *Sun Tzu, Star Chinese General and Military Strategist of Antiquity*

As I was preparing to start a workshop several years ago, and speaking with a coach, I pointed out a youth participant who had just walked into the room. I identified his slouched posture and posed the question, "What has happened in his short life for him to hold himself so forlornly?"

I told the coach that if I did nothing more in the workshop than have this young man walking straight and tall by the end, I would have succeeded in helping him in ways beyond our imaginings, in his game and otherwise in his life. I remember how he progressed over the course of the workshop, slowly but surely gaining his full height, and how tall he was walking by the end of the workshop. I felt good about his chances in the upcoming national competition — and in life.

Posture is the Window to Your State of Mind

A person's posture is a clear window to their state of mind, and probably their soul. As you may have discovered thus far, when you change past memories with tools like FUSING and TALENT MODE, the result is a strong and very powerful posture. In this chapter, we will further develop and strengthen your ability to maintain this kind of posture. In doing so, it will not only prevent NO-Zone thoughts from entering your head but will also help you to get rid of them whenever they do.

NO-Zone thoughts thrive when you have a slumped or depressed posture. When you run or walk briskly and your posture straightens, you'll find it very difficult to have a rounded back or slumped shoulders, or the negative thoughts that accompany them. And with that change, depressed moods vanish. So, instead of a traditional therapeutic approach of talking about problems over many hours and days, we need an approach that simply changes our posture and allows that to dictate how we feel.

Slumped Posture Equals Weakness

Several years ago I had a neighbor who was a promising, young hockey player. I would occasionally notice him walking to school, a forlorn sight, head tilted forward, shoulders rounded, eyes fixed just a few feet in front of him on the sidewalk. Based on his posture, I wondered what negative thoughts were swirling around in his mind: "I hate school." "I didn't do my homework." "I hate my teachers." "My girlfriend is too clingy." "My parents are stupid." And add his five-minute walk to the five hours of his school day and you can make some pretty accurate predictions about his performance in hockey that evening. It is going to suffer.

Any person hunched over like this is at a disadvantage, even before the start of a game. The lungs are trapped in tight, constricted compartments and breathing is labored. The spine is compressed, reducing the effectiveness of the nervous system and the signals it needs to send. Muscles are tight, making them slow, inefficient and weak. Now, many athletes resolve this kind of posture through the physical exertion and excitement of the game. But by then, in most sports anyway, it produces an incredible waste of opportunity.

Simple shifts in posture affect us dramatically. I demonstrate this in workshops by having a participant hold his forearm above his head, forming a protective karate-type block. I stare directly in his eyes and press down on the arm hard — which usually meets total resistance. Then I have him avoid my gaze and look at the floor. I press down again but with only one of my fingers — and there is usually no resistance. If a simple downward glance like this can wreak this kind of havoc, you can imagine the degree of weakness you create when you slouch. Experience this karate block exercise with a partner; it is eye opening.

For optimum power and energy, you need to keep your head and eyes straight ahead and your posture erect. Simply by doing this, the strength and power you'll possess in your game will be amazing. With the next exercise called POWER WALK, you can resolve and prevent deflated postures, no matter how tough a competition gets.

Exercise: POWER WALK

1) Set up a runway A to B (see example below), about fifteen feet long without any obstructions (use a large room, hallway or yard). Stand in the middle — Point C —and think about a NO-Zone problem, preferably one that causes your posture to slump.

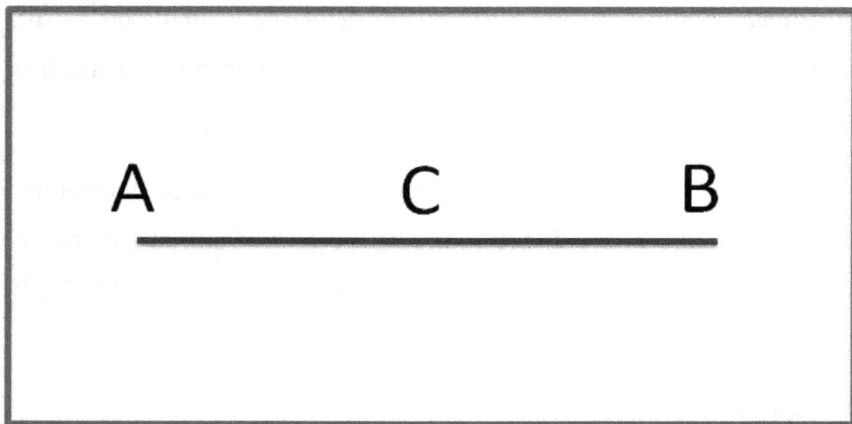

```
A              C         B
_____
```

2) Walk to Point A on the runway, and "leave" the problem image of you at Point C. Looking at the Point C image, notice how that "YOU" needs some coaching. Especially notice the posture.

3) Now, walk powerfully with an imaginary "sky hook" pulling your head erect so that you can feel your spine elongate. Walking with a comfortable stride, and with some speed, make several passes back and forth from A to B.

4) After several powerful passes through C, stop at Point C and think about your problem. If it is pretty much gone, you've been successful. If not, continue with several more passes.

POWER WALK can be used to resolve almost any NO-Zone experience from the fear of competition to the embarrassment of a meltdown. It is especially good at getting rid of self-talk — any self-talk. Try pacing back and forth before a competition as a simple means of warding off pre-competition nerves. The implications of creating and maintaining your Zone via a strong posture can be seen in everyday professional sports — strong, upright, powerful and intimidating — no matter what the score. As a competitive athlete, you need to make it yours.

Starting today, walk powerfully whether practicing or competing, and at work and school. It feels good; it keeps self-talk at bay and it makes for an efficient use of energy (in the eyes especially). Lastly, it can be a powerful intimidating factor when seen by your opponents.

Chapter Summary

So, whether you use POWER WALK as a means to fix NO-Zone memories that weaken you, to prepare for a competition, or to ensure an intimidating air, it can make you feel ten feet tall and help you to perform accordingly. More interestingly, just as a simple exercise like POWER WALK can make you feel larger than life, in the next chapter we'll make net openings, golf fairways and baseballs, etc. seem fantastically huge as well.

POWER WALK in Action: Triathlon

❝ I was new at triathlon but was good at the three events — swimming, cycling and running. Swimming is my best event, which is even better, as I had always heard that well-trained swimmers had an advantage over those who were primarily cyclists or runners. So when I felt my first panic attack regarding the mass start of the swim, my world was rocked. You may have seen the wild stampede of hundreds of bodies hitting the water all at once. My sudden and unexpected panic with respect to it had me looking for solutions — and I found it in this System, particularly with POWER WALK.

In one go, I put that panicky image of me in the middle of my hallway, got into my 'Zone' walk, and marched back and forth through the image. In about five minutes, I was able to think through the start of the swim event with no panic at all. And in the next event, even when someone elbowed me in face, I actually felt my Zone grow even stronger. ❞

— Triathlete

18 Now You See It...Now You Don't

When I'm anxious on the golf green, I'm putting to a thimble. But when I'm in the Zone, it's a basket.

"A five-goal scorer can tell you the brand name of the pad of every goalie in the league. I'm seeing the net, he's seeing the pad."

—Wayne Gretzky, Star Hockey Player

Most of us will have days when our game "goes south". Our friends hit fairways, swish basketballs, find minute cracks in goaltenders pads and we can't. Except on occasion. In that game we too succeed in all parts of our game, until the next outing, when it is back to square one. We search for solutions to ensure success such as eyewear or more practice time, or come up with excuses such as dim light, background distractions or no sleep. But, more often than not, we fail because we lose the Zone and it can nullify all our training and experience in the blink of an eye by dulling our senses, particularly our vision.

Narrow Focus, Fast Game

When we are frustrated, down on our luck or highly stressed, our vision contracts and becomes much narrower in its focus. (There is a great article on why this might happen entitled: *The Reptilian Brain, Dissociation and Seeing from the Core*, by Rosemary Gaddum Gordon.) Quite literally, our eye muscles freeze and the image is seen less clearly. The contrast in lighting can trick the eye more easily. Items in the foreground and background can take on greater visual significance. Other senses are affected as well. Noises may seem louder and people's voices may seem more obnoxious. Your equipment may not have the same comfort. Overall, our brains can be a lot "noisier" and more scattered and, as a result, our intended target can seem to be a lot smaller than normal.

Contrast this to days when we feel very good and are in the Zone. All our senses are processing information smoothly and efficiently. Our intended target seems so easy to hit. People and other distractions disappear. Our equipment is an extension of our bodies and there is no thinking, no second-guessing. It just happens, sometimes so vividly that we get the sense of having an out-of-body experience. The clarity is amazing.

Training Our Brain

If there is any reoccurring theme in this book, it is that our brains have an amazing ability to learn, no matter what our age, by fine-tuning and developing our senses. In this case, we need to train it to see our intended target better, whether a net, a spot on the tennis court or an actual target. The key is the word *train*. We want to train our brains to see only the image we want — that of our intended target — not the background of people, colors, goaltenders or other opponents. We want to train our brains to make the process of seeing and hitting the target so easy that our body does it automatically.

Our brains take in and store information based on the excitement and enjoyment level of an event. For example, if you have been to an enjoyable concert, your memory of the performance will tend to appear large, bright and loud in your mind's eye — memorable. And, if you have been to a terrible concert (or a dull lecture) your memory of the performance is more likely indistinct, small and barely audible — forgettable. Being able to assess the difference in concerts is of little importance, except that your memory works the same way with your intended target. The unpleasant stress you felt all those days when you struggled to get a handle on that target is etched in your brain. And the opposite is also true, as in your moments of brilliance you owned it.

So, being able to identify the good days and figure out and use "GOOD-DAY" strategies would be very useful. And that is what we'll do via VISTA, an amazing tool that enhances our perceptual ability.

Exercise: VISTA

VISTA is designed to teach you (and your brain) to shuck off visual distractions and lock onto your intended target fast. The word "VISTA" means "to see the big picture" and that is exactly what we want it to be — BIG. This exercise gives you GPS on how your brain typically sees the intended image — small and dark, perhaps — so that you can make changes to enlarge and brighten it up.

No-Zone experiences, where we missed our intended target, will typically have weak images that are hard to see, fuzzy and fast, as you can well imagine, or you would never have missed them. Zone experiences will typically be the exact opposite where our intended target is large and clear. This information gives you the 'big picture" of how your brain perceives both your NO-Zone and Zone experiences. And, with VISTA, you get the opportunity to use that information to make changes.

To do that, you will need to mentally review your best memory and use it as a template (ideal example) of swishing baskets in basketball, one-stroke putting in golf, scoring an ace in tennis, a personal best in track, a winning goal in hockey, etc. And then, you will apply this template to all aspects of your game, especially where your ideal target is hard to see.

1) The Problematic Image

We are going to start with how your brain has stored the information about your hard-to-see image — a NO-Zone image if you will. It is a net, goal, or location on the court that frustrates and embarrasses you when you miss, often inexplicably. Imagine this intended target as you would in your game. Does it appear:

- Focused or unfocused?
- Dark or bright?
- In color or black and white?
- Contained (intended target in tunnel vision) or peripheral (intended target in whole scene)?
- Near or far?

There may be similarities with other people as to how you perceive these images, but your perception will be distinct to you. As a guide, your GPS for this NO-Zone image might be seeing the intended target as dark, unfocused, black and white, contained, and distant.

2) The Super, Clear Image

This is the type of image you love. This is how your brain processes intended targets that feel easy to hit. People admire this kind of precision. It is your Zone template. Imagine this kind of image in your game. Does it appear:

- Focused or unfocused?
- Dark or bright?
- In color or black and white?
- Contained (intended target in tunnel vision) or peripheral (intended target in whole scene)?
- Near or far?

Keep in mind that your list will be distinctive to you, and the visual qualities are the ones you will use as your template. As a guide, your GPS for this kind of Zone template might be seeing the intended target as bright, focused, colorful, peripheral and close.

3) What's Dark Becomes Bright

Compare the lists you created, as they will give you some insight into how your brain has captured and stored information regarding the NO-Zone and Zone memories. Now, in your mind's eye:

a) Place the NO-Zone target image (small golf hole on the green, small basketball net, huge goaltender with no net openings, etc.) dead center in front of you.

b) Physically reach both your hands straight out — don't be shy — and grab the image like you would grab someone by the shoulders. Now stretch the image apart by slowly moving your arms outward to your sides. As you do this, visually add all the qualities of your Zone template. Splash it with some color, stretch it out, make it huge, brighten it up and zero in on it. Be creative; make it crystal clear.

c) Once you've stretched out your arms as wide as you can, close your hands to the center in front of you. Pull the image apart a second time, but a little faster and with even more of the Zone qualities. Do this process five to ten times over and over, faster and faster.

d) Now think back to the original problematic target in your game. It has probably changed in your perception. If not, redo the exercise and make it even brighter and clearer and sharper, depending of course on your Zone template image.

Test It Out

With VISTA, you can transform your perception of virtually any component of your game: your intended target, the venue, the weather, equipment, etc. (I've even had athletes use this concept to enhance their academic studies by imagining textbooks as Sports Illustrated or computer games.) With this kind of change in perspective, you can practically predict the end result. However, if you can see your intended target as huge and clear and you're still missing it, it's probably time to adjust your technique, replace your equipment or meet with your coach to improve your technique. For beginners who have no memories of excellence, use your experiences in other sports.

Ask most competitive athletes and they'll have games where their intended target is easy to hit. Like them, on these good days, when all these stars are aligned, you will have the corresponding Zone FEEL and hit everything. On the bad days, when the stars are misaligned, you will have the NO-Zone FEEL and truly feel the world is against you. VISTA can help you to re-align the stars.

Chapter Summary

Practice VISTA to transform your ability to see your target by copying and applying your moments of brilliance — big, slow, sharp and bright images. Use it as a regular part of your routine to fix problematic aspects of your game or as a warm-up before heading out to your play. To others, it looks like you're shaking off the "cobwebs," but only you will know that you're enhancing the image of your intended target. In the next chapter, we'll take your visional acuity a step further and train your eyes to snap to your intended target acutely and instantly.

VISTA in Action: Triathlon

❝ If you have ever trained for an open-water swimming event, you'll know that the pool will only help you so far, namely with your technique, stamina and efficiency. I can handle the scrum at the start as well as cold water. But when I was approaching an open-water swim in the ocean, this really freaked me out, especially in Australia, a place renowned for currents and other things! VISTA came in handy here. I used my experiences of many lake swims to transform the ocean. Ultimately, on competition day, I stayed in my Zone and the swim felt as comfortable as any I'd had in a freshwater lake. **❞**

— Triathlete

19   A Lesson from Waldo

Visual acuity is either your Achilles' heel
or your ace in the hole.

"I like going out shooting those tough conditions because typically
[other] athletes let it get to them and change up their routine
and slip up and miss a few targets."

— *Vincent Hancock, Star Olympic Skeet Shooter*

Perception plays a huge role in all sports. In hockey and soccer, for example, it is typical for average caliber players to perceive goaltenders as difficult to beat. And they can be so visually absorbed with the image of the goaltender that the goaltender becomes the target rather than the opening surrounding the goaltender. For these players, goal scoring becomes a two-step process where the athlete sees (1) the goaltender, and then (2) the opening. Elite athletes use a one step process and see *only* the net openings.

It is the same for football quarterbacks, where the two-step process involves seeing (1) the coverage of the opponents and then (2) the pass receiver. When this happens, the usual excuse is that the receivers were difficult to see and "nobody" was in the clear. However, even with the tightest coverage, there is usually someone open. Some quarterbacks can hit any receiver, regardless of the conditions and regardless of the background. And if you ask them why, they might even tell you that it is intuitive. But it is really their ability to see their intended target in one step, not two.

What's Good for Wartime Gunners

For athletes who complain about distractions, training can help to eliminate the distractions and get one's eyes to snap to your target. In wartime London, gunners were taught to recognize aircraft shapes instantly. The searchlights might only catch a momentary flash of an aircraft and they had to know instantly if it was one of their own or the enemy (Derek Balmer, *Verbal rendition from survivor of London blitzkrieg*). That is exactly what you need to do — instantly see your target.

A great book that can be used to train your eyes for this purpose is probably one you would never think of. It is a children's book series about a character called *Waldo*, by Martin Handford. The purpose of this book is to find the Waldo character in a profusion of colorful drawings. But to describe it, fails to do it justice. Take a moment to sneak a copy from your child or grandchild or purchase the book. Most editions of the book are excellent and it is worth acquiring for the following visual acuity drill (and for reading to your children or grandchildren). It is complex and challenging enough to keep you happily engaged for hours. It gives you a rare opportunity to train your visual acuity to very high levels.

Visual Acuity with a Mental Snapshot

Once you have a *Where's Waldo?* book, it is a fairly simple process to find the Waldo character — in seconds. The trick is to (1) stare at the initial example of Waldo on the first page, (2) create a mental snapshot of the image so that you get very familiar with it, and, (3) effortlessly scan each page of the book to find him. As you engage your subconscious mind in the process, the image of Waldo will eventually "jump" off the page at you in a rather quick and surprising manner.

The images on successive *Where's Waldo* pages get more and more convoluted and confusing, yet it becomes surprisingly possible to find each image of Waldo with increasing speed. Once you have found Waldo on all the pages, you can use the same process to find other images. And, once you have experimented with this for a while, and have found the easy-to-find figures, you can search for the tiniest images, whatever that particular Waldo book offers you.

In the book I had saved after my own children had outgrown it, I experimented with how fast I could find the image of Waldo. It was easy, so I challenged myself to find a tiny toothpick-sized shape that had a dab of red on it — the image of a scroll. Initially I sectioned off the page into a grid pattern and painstakingly explored each section. No luck, but lots of frustration.

I was unsure where to turn next and decided that my level of frustration — the symptom of my failing to find the scroll — was merely GPS. So I used VISTA to resolve the frustration, as well as FUSING and TALENT MODE, and then went back to my search. This time I perceived tiny images with bits of white and red — probably well-designed decoys, I'm sure, and I felt my frustration grow again — more GPS.

Getting Closer

I resolved the frustration and, in the ensuing search, out popped many more little decoys interspersed amongst the pictures, which brought me to a new level of frustration. Once more — after which I vowed to quit this colossal waste of time — I used the frustration as GPS and the scroll jumped off the page, just like that.

So I can hear you now, "How does finding Waldo or a scroll help me to hit my intended target?" Well, no matter what sport you play or at what level you play it, finding Waldo amongst the distracting images is the same process whereby your brain finds the intended target among the background images, whether you are a soccer player finding the net (versus the goaltender) or a football linebacker reading the play. If you can learn to eliminate myriad distracting colors while finding Waldo, you can learn to eliminate background noise and distractions and find your intended target instantly.

In the past you may have excused your misses as the result of lack of light, colorful (and loud) spectators or other distractions. Now, as certainly as you found Waldo in a profusion of background colors, you can teach your brain to locate your target, under just about any conditions.

The key to creating heightened visual acuity and locking onto your target is to train your brain to subconsciously make the distractions irrelevant. Your "Waldo" skills can be used in the same way wartime gunners picked out enemy aircraft:

1) Engrain the picture of your intended target in your mind;

2) Use the concept of GPS to stay in the Zone by eliminating frustration or other blocks;

3) Allow your subconscious mind to find that target for you. Instantly.

VISTA in Action: Surfing

66 The beautiful thing about surfing is that you can look out your window and see the conditions and waves and make a decision as to whether to go or not. When the waves are great, you surf, and when they are not you go to the gym and train there. But when you are on the World Surfing Tour, waves don't always cooperate. You have to take what you get and it can get very frustrating surfing mushy waves that allow maybe one quick trick, if that.

VISTA proved to be one of the best exercises as it allowed me to treat mushy waves with the same aggressiveness as I treated good waves. As a result, I milked them for what they were worth and got the highest score possible with no frustration. The *Where's Waldo* exercise, on the other hand, trained me to get very good at picking out the best of the "worst" waves before anyone else did. **99**

— Surfer

Chapter Summary

You have now turned finding your intended target into a one-step process by training your brain through the help of a children's book. In the next chapter you'll shift from changing your perspective of the intended target to changing your perspective of another form of distraction — people. You'll learn to fix intimidating, frustrating and distracting behavior by making it a one-step process as well. Okay, maybe a three-step process, as people can really get under your skin.

20 Mind Coach

If there weren't any people to distract me,
I'd play really well.

"Find your own picture, your own self in anything that goes bad.
It's awfully easy to blame your coach or your teammates, but if it's
bad, and you're keen on being a leader, you're responsible. If your
teammate makes a mistake, you did it. You're accepting
leadership. A bad practice, a bad game, it's up to you, the athlete
leader on your team, to assume your responsibility."

— Paul "Bear" Bryant, Star Football Coach
(as paraphrased by Bob Palmer)

Imagine how different your current athletic performance would be if your past was only filled with successful experiences. That being unlikely, imagine changing every bad experience you have ever had into a positive one so that you create a sense of having had no bad experiences. No matter what was on the line, no matter what the conditions, you would have only positive memories to draw on. As far back in your memory bank as you cared to look, there would be only the good, the strong and the powerful. This is the SportExcel System. All the exercises learned thus far, from Zone FEEL to VISTA, are all designed to displace and override the NO-Zone blocks that cause you to falter.

The People Problem

Imagine how different your current athletic performance would be if your past experiences were only you and the game — no coaches, parents or bullies. How much more pleasant the game would be with no one attempting to outsmart you, to distract you with tantrums, to intimidate you with their prowess or dictate to you "their way or they highway".

That being unlikely, you might ask, can I change my perception of my opponents — the good, the bad and the challenging — so that they disappear as well? Yes, not exactly the Tony Soprano-style of disappearing, but certainly at the conscious level. We all have people distractions. They can be coaches, wives, husbands, bosses or children/parents; they can be competitors or officials; they can be spectators or the lack of spectators. People do a lot of things to mess us up, both deliberately and inadvertently. However, the truth be known, most of the time we have only ourselves to blame. We let them into our lives — and our heads — and can just as easily learn to get them out.

A cartoon I often refer to shows a psychiatrist in a chair with his client on the couch. The client complains that his mother always pushes his buttons. The psychiatrist replies that of course she does — because *she installed them.* But for us it doesn't matter who installed them. We own the buttons that get pushed and it is up to us to de-install them, just as we do with obsolete programs on our computers.

Make Opponents Beatable

The "de-install" approach is the same for any number of athletic disciplines. In the sport of hockey, it is often the goalie that intimidates the opposition by appearing huge and imposing. Making goalies "beatable" has huge implications for the morale of a team. In baseball, it is the pitcher to the batter or the batter to the pitcher. How one perceives the other can give an incredible edge in the standoff. In coaching, how the coach perceives the athletes and how the athletes perceive the coach can be motivating or de-motivating. In figure skating, as in other sports, the prospect of performing in front of a crowd can make or break a performance. In all sports, the intimidation factor of both coaches and other athletes can be huge.

The Psych-out

There is a golf "psych-out" book called: *How to Win at Golf Without Actually Playing Well*, by Jon Winokur. I flipped through it in the bookstore and left it on the shelf because it was so different from my leadership approach to winning. I realize now that the book is worth buying for one very good reason — it is an education as to the kind of mind games athletes can face

A "psych-out" is based upon our amazing ability to make mountains out of molehills, or, in people terms, giants out of normal people. In karate, for example, I was always amazed by one of my instructors who always looked so big and tall, and yet when I stood beside him he might have been only a half-inch taller. As he was an amazing fighter, and a number of belt levels higher than I was, I considered myself fortunate not to have to fight him in a competition.

Many athletes have the necessary technical skills, but at the subconscious level envision themselves as less significant or even insignificant when comparing themselves to other athletes and, as a result, are easily intimidated and defeated by presence rather than skill. These athletes need to step back and get a new perspective on the situation. How many times have coaches (or parents or teachers) suggested that we cool down and count to ten, or step back and open our eyes to how our opponent is taunting, teasing or otherwise irritating us? How can coaches see this but not us? Well, there *is* no good reason, and with a tool called MIND COACH you'll become your own coach.

Exercise: MIND COACH

1) Think of a competitor (we'll call him John) who negatively affects your game.

2) Imagine you are in a theatre. The stage lights come up on one side of the stage and John appears. Pick one word that describes his behavior — no swear words please. In this example, we'll call him "intimidating."

3) Now notice stage lights come up on the other side of the stage, and you are looking at YOU. Pick a word that describes YOU on stage in the context of competing against John. How about "nervous?"

4) Now, ask yourself the question, "Who is leading whom?" Is John leading YOU or vice versa? I believe you'll find that indeed it is John who is leading you, whether he realizes it or not.

5) To get on the *leader*board, you'll have to take leadership. So, in your mind's eye, go down to the YOU on stage. Put that YOU in the Zone, make him ten feet tall. Make him absolutely invincible.

6) And lastly, step into the shoes of that YOU on stage and feel that new strength, power and confidence. Take one more look at John and you'll notice that he too may have changed — diminished perhaps? Now go test out your newfound leadership skill — and notice how John reacts to it.

Don't Trust Anyone

A while ago, I watched as that same karate instructor I mentioned earlier lost to an opponent he should have beaten easily. A few months later I cornered him at a Christmas party and asked him what had happened. He told me that he too was puzzled. I asked him if he wanted to find out. He gave me a puzzled look and said yes. So I then took him through the MIND COACH exercise to give him some insight and had him go back to the memory of the competition. He immediately started to laugh. What did you notice? I asked. He didn't beat me in the ring, he said. He beat me in the warm up. I never talk to anyone before a match and he came up to me and mocked me, in what at the time seemed a humorous vein. My karate instructor laughed again, and I could tell by the laugh that no one was going to find that chink in his armor again.

The 30-Minute Rule

In the sports world, as I inferred in previous chapters, it is common for players and even coaches to subtly give advice, create doubt or plant suggestions right before a competition. MIND COACH is essential here, as this has prevented many of my athletes from falling into the same trap. However, one tip is to stay away from everyone a good 30 or more minutes before your competition to prevent people from getting inside your head — period — because, believe me, some are very good at it. I call it *"The 30-Minute Rule."* Use the time to get into your Zone, rehearse your competition with your DÉJÀ-VU DVD and take on all comers with MIND COACH. Take my advice, "Don't trust anyone!"

MIND COACH in Action: Volleyball

" I had an elementary-school coach who tried to motivate us on the court by yelling at us. And, although he didn't scare me, his yelling pulled all of us out of the Zone. In preparation for one particular game, I used MIND COACH and imagined myself twice as big as the coach. Then I planned to always plant myself between he and my teammates in order to shield them. That next game, once he'd yelled his advice (at my face), I turned back to the girls in my best Zone, and smiled. It worked well that game and for the remainder of the season, as we rarely lost a beat and ended up winning the school championship. At the end of the season, the coach came up to me and thanked me for my leadership. I smiled and shrugged, as I believe he might have caught on to what I had been doing! **"** — Volleyball Player

Chapter Summary

The applications for MIND COACH are endless and can be applied to all areas of your life — from taking leadership to building relationships to dealing with bullies in school. Practice it just like the other tools and you will find yourself minimizing the negative effect that opponents, audiences, parents and coaches have on you. Become sensitized to the fact that athletes and their coaches will attempt to psych you out, whether intentionally or unintentionally. Refuse to play that kind of game. Instead, call them on it if necessary or simply use MIND COACH to fix it and move on. In the next two chapters, we learn how coaches and parents can use the same exercise for building leadership, learning new skills and developing coaching/parenting strategies.

21 The Coach as Emotional Ballast

That kid will never win a karate competition —
Oops, did Sensei Bob just say that?

"A good coach will make his players see what they can be,
rather than what they are."

— Ara Parseghian, Star Football Coach

As a high performance trainer, I work with baseball pitchers who throw wildly in critical situations, when, just moments before, they were throwing strikes; volleyball players who, in game situations, act as if they have forgotten all the drills they have been practicing; and swimmers whose times are much slower in competition than their personal bests in practice. In most sports it is called choking, a phenomenon that every athlete has probably experienced at least once. As frustrating as it is, it is easy to fix, especially in an athlete's early years since it is likely a coach who has caused it in the first place.

Now, if you are a coach, please don't be embarrassed if you "resemble" this comment, and certainly take your fingers off the keyboard regarding "a letter to the author" complaining to me. If it helps any, I say this because it is the caring side of coaches that gets them in trouble. Most coaches are very passionately concerned for their athletes' wellbeing and they cause their athletes to falter precisely because of it.

That GPS Sinking Feeling

As a coach, when one of my karate students made a mistake and lost a match, I would generally feel their angst (GPS) through a sinking feeling in *my* stomach. This very real connection — this direct pathway between coach and athlete — is what makes us caring and compassionate individuals. But at the same time, when we feel an athlete's disappointment it can also make us less than effective coaches. Why? They see and especially feel our concern but have no way of telling the difference between our disappointment *for* them, and perceived disappointment *in* them.

Too Much Empathy

As coaches we need that empathy for our athletes, but we also need to know how and when to turn it off. Rather than follow our athletes into whatever state they get into, we need to exert leadership. I call this role 'the emotional coach', where at any time, no matter what troubling thoughts an athlete is thinking, he or she can always turn to the coach and feel the coach's Zone. Yes, the Zone. Watch high school sports games and you'll see coaches screaming at refs, gesturing disappointedly at players and generally carrying on with unsportsmanlike displays. So you can understand know why athletes expect the opposite. It is disastrous for personal and team morale —and that is so wrong.

To mirror back to athletes their worst fears of failure, frustration and disappointment is to confirm that they should be disappointed. They have failed, so they must accept that they are failures. Worse yet, it is almost as if we are trying to ingrain and reinforce that they acted stupidly so that each time they step back in the game they will remember to (never) mess up again. It is a less than favorable approach, as it actually encourages thinking about past mistakes.

As coaches, we need to stay in the Zone and avoid reinforcing their expectations of a negative response. When they make a mistake, turn to us to have it confirmed and get a powerful Zone reaction instead, imagine the bewilderment. And that bewilderment — brought about by the athlete's seeing and mirroring *our* Zone — allows him or her to recover spectacularly fast and get right back into the game. It is very cool to watch. Two teams can make the same number of mistakes and it will be the team that recovers the quickest from mistakes that will win. This kind of coaching approach encourages that kind of fast recovery.

To stay in the Zone as a coach is to believe that athletes have to:

- Develop the resources that are required to thrive on pressure;
- Experience losing in order to build resilience;
- Experience intimidation in order to counter it;
- Deal effectively with losing in order to become a champion;
- Observe the coach as a role model of how to handle adversity;
- Develop a work ethic and create a powerful Zone.

That said, here is my Number One rule in coaching:

If I stay in the Zone, my athletes will.

As coaches we have to draw on our own personal history of skills and strategies to model the kinds of behaviors we expect of athletes. Remember — and we often forget this — competition is wholly new to young athletes and whatever impression it makes on them can last their entire lives. The coaches who understand this rule (about staying in the Zone for their athletes) are often delightfully amazed by the effectiveness of adding this one approach to their skillset.

Exercise Revisited: MIND COACH

For a coach, being your athletes' emotional ballast can be a lot of fun. For many coaches, it is both a physical and a philosophical shift — but we have to have easy and practical ways to implement the change. In the previous chapter I introduced you to MIND COACH. Here it is in a coach's version:

1) Think of an athlete (we'll call him John Jr.) who struggles at competitions.

2) Imagine you're in a theatre where the stage lights come up and reveal John Jr. Pick a word that describes his behavior. For this example, we'll call him "scared".

3) Now notice that a spotlight has come up on the other side of the stage and there is an image of you, the coach. Pick a word that describes the YOU on stage. We'll label him "concerned."

4) Now, ask the question, "Who is leading whom?" I think you'll find John Jr. is in full control of your emotions, inadvertently, I'm sure. But since you are the coach and the leader, you might want to take back leadership. So in your mind's eye, go down to the

YOU on stage. Put that YOU in the Zone — ten feet tall and inspiringly powerful;

5) And lastly, step into the shoes of that YOU and feel that new strength, power and confidence. Then take a peek at John Jr. He could possibly be looking very "ready to play". Of course, now you'll want to test out if this is really as effective a coaching tool as it sounds.

Over my 20 years of teaching karate, I frequently used MIND COACH to tailor my coaching style. One particular student I'll call Mary was a case in point. She typically came to class in a disheveled uniform, and an attitude that I took to mean, "Just you try to teach me anything." Even in her first class, I thought, "She'll never survive." And following the typical "oops, did I say that?" I plugged her into MIND COACH and continued teaching. I certainly had no idea of how I was going to make her karate career a success, but, after doing the exercise only once, I could feel the passion that I would require.

Mary's transformation was slow and steady after that. She formed friendships with other classmates and even started to attend tournaments. Of course, the other students consistently came back with trophies, and Mary always stood out in those pictures, the odd one out, with no trophy. She just lacked something I couldn't put my finger on and again I caught myself saying: *"That kid will never win a karate competition. Oops."* Once again MIND COACH came to the rescue.

And then it happened. Mary was in the finals of point sparring at the national championship. I could taste the medal — a first or second guaranteed — and the only way Mary could lose was to hit her opponent in the face and get disqualified... which she did. My shoulders sagged and my heart went out to her, but I quickly recovered my Zone so that we could make the best of it. But when the officials presented the medals for kata forms first, Mary received the bronze — and she had her first medal. She beamed; I beamed. And believe me, the celebration that ensued produced more than a few tears and still stirs up my emotions when I tell the story today.

More often than not, helping athletes such as Mary get the most out of their performance is simply a matter of knowing that you can. It is your ability to step back via MIND COACH and create a new perspective. You get to see how your leadership behaviors — both good and bad — affect the behaviors of your athletes. And it gives you a second, third and perhaps infinite chance to get it right. Give it a shot and see how much you can increase your enjoyment in the game, as well as that of your athletes.

Chapter Summary

MIND COACH ensures that your athletes stay in the Zone no matter what mistakes they make. The only meaning for "choke" they will know is gagging on food. MIND COACH is the rehearsal that will keep you and your athlete on target. You are helping them perform — and YOU will need to put on the best performance of THEIR lives. And, if you are a parent (or even a grandparent, boss, etc.) who thinks the same kind of approach could work for you, the next chapter will include you in the game as well.

MIND COACH in Action: Volleyball

❝ Bob changed the way I coach my volleyball players. I had a very talented group of senior boys one year. They had height, athleticism and smarts, but they would still collapse from time to time. When I first talked to Bob by phone, he asked what typically causes my players to fall apart. There is no explanation, I said, and that is why I called you. "Who supports the boys when they collapse?" Bob asked. "Would it be their teammates on the bench?" No, I said, as they typically collapse too. "Would it be their opponents?" he asked. I laughed. "Would it be their fans?" I laughed again, only a bit more sheepishly, as I knew the next question. "What are you doing when they are collapsing?" he asked. At that point I had the image of me sitting on the bench with my face in my hands. Oops, I said and I described the image. "I think I can help you," Bob said. **❞**

— Volleyball Coach

22   The Parents: A Coach's Best Ally

Take your ear buds out and talk to me about the competition — I drove you, didn't I?

"Leadership [parenthood] is a matter of having people [your kids] look at you and gain confidence, seeing how you react. If you're in control, they're in control."

— Tom Landry, Star Football Coach
(as paraphrased by Bob Palmer)

In the previous chapter I wrote on the topic of coaches being the ballast for their athletes and the incredible results they could get from this simple philosophical shift. I purposefully neglected to describe one of the key players in the process — parents. I'm very supportive of parents of young athletes because I was one, and I know what they go through. They spend more time with the athlete than the coach and yet often feel undervalued by both the coach and the athlete. They also get blamed for the many behavioral sins of their child.

The main way parents find to get around this is to stay home. Another is to watch the event covertly from behind a pillar or tree. This chapter is aimed at parents who wish to overcome this stigma and actually be a benefit to both the coach and their child.

Coach Greevy's Camp

When I first started working with Coach Les Greevy's Olympic Development Team in Pennsylvania, the parents of his athletes were having challenges with their children. The athlete would make a mistake and feel bad and the parent would feel bad as well. The child would further collapse and cry and the parent would have tears welling up in their eyes as well. This emotional loop between child and parent would spiral downward out of control with mom (or dad) in the stands in an agonized, emotional dance with the child on the field. And they were only doing what parents do well, empathizing with their child.

So, here is parenting rule number one:

If I stay in the Zone, my child will.

Sound similar to the coach's rule in Chapter 20?

To help resolve the dynamic between parent and child, Coach Greevy borrowed time from our athlete workshop to address the issue with the parents. I treated them like coaches, told them that they could no longer be spectators and introduced the golden rule.

Parents Are NOT Spectators

"What do you mean we can't just be spectators?" was one parent's response.   I told them that they *could* be spectators and follow the emotional ebb and flow of their children's performance, or they could be emotional coaches and remain in the Zone (leadership) for all the ups and downs of any competitive activity.   No matter where you sit, I added, your child will locate you.   And when they do, your Zone can influence them in exciting and powerful ways.

To emphasize this point, I described an athlete who mostly traveled to competitions with his family.   One time he traveled with his dad, another time with an aunt or an uncle.   Occasionally he traveled with his coach.   Over the course of several tournaments a pattern developed: When he traveled with his family he performed horribly, at least in the initial rounds of competition, and when he traveled with his coach, he performed well and even won a national collegiate competition.

I told the parents that the trip with his family was superficially about the competition, and mostly about sightseeing and expectations, squabbles, grandma's troubles, the cost of the sport, the price of gas and the business call on the cell phone.   On the other hand, the trip with his coach was all about competitions, stories of success, stories about fellowship, stories about all manner of things related to the sport.   In this light, the latter experience with the coach wires the athlete's mental circuitry for success.

Parents Are Emotional Coaches

At this point I could tell that the parents were concerned. How could they compete with any coach? I told them to not even try. They did not have the technical skills or experiences that relate to becoming a coach. But they did have the maturity and life experiences that relate to becoming an Emotional Coach.

I told them that I was an Emotional Coach with my daughter the equestrian. Now, I know very little about the sport except that horses are big and unpredictable. But I would watch her ride and see her make mistakes that made no sense after all of her years of lessons. So in one of these lessons it occurred to me that I might be a part (a big part) of the problem. I left the stable, went to my car and took myself through the MIND COACH exercise. What I visualized shocked me. I could only see my daughter spinning in circles on the horse. I was scared for her safety, and I realized that my fear must have been having an incredible impact on her performance. Some insight. With it, I (Emotional Coach Dad) quickly fixed the spinning, at least in my mind, got in the Zone and returned to watch my daughter. And, to my amazement, the rest of the training session was spectacular. No more issues with cadence. Wow. My fear clearly had had a huge impact her.

The parents smiled knowingly.

Exercise Revisited: MIND COACH for Parents

1) Think of your child (we'll call him J.J.) who keeps his ear buds in and doesn't want to talk before, during or after competitions.

2) Imagine you're in a theatre where the stage lights come up and reveal J.J. Pick a word that describes his behavior. For this example, we'll call him "inconsiderate."

3) Now notice that a spotlight has come up on the other side of the stage and there is an image of you. Pick a word that describes the YOU on stage. We'll call him/her "angry."

4) Now, ask the question, "Who is leading whom?" I think you'll find J.J. is in full control of your emotions, inadvertently, I'm sure. But since you are the parent and the leader (and have years of emotional self-control), you might want to take back leadership. So, in your mind's eye, go down to the YOU on stage. Put that YOU in the Zone — ten feet tall and inspiring.

5) And lastly, step into the shoes of that YOU and feel that new strength, power and confidence. Then take a peek at J.J. He could possibly be looking like he wants to talk about the competition. Of course, now you'll want to test out to see if this is really as effective a parenting tool as it sounds.

Communicating with your child is a big challenge, but the parents who have adopted this perspective rave about the positive effect it has had on their family. As parents, you naturally spend an inordinate amount of time being chauffeurs to your kids, so you might as well use this time with them in mind instead of conducting business on the cell phone or mindlessly listening to the radio. The Zone is contagious. Twenty minutes seated beside you with your full attention will be energizing for your child. An hour will be dazzling. One hockey parent has been using this approach for several years to get his son in the Zone before his skates hit the ice. And last I heard the kid is now a professional.

Chapter Summary

With MIND COACH, you have a powerful leadership tool to get your child ready for practices and competitions — Zone ready. When you hand over your young athlete — in the Zone — to his or her coach, the coach will love you for it. And, by using MIND COACH to create a strong emotional ballast for all your kids' activities, you will help them to build confidence, self-esteem and skill for life. They might even want to talk to you. One of the ingredients you'll be evoking to get them ready is adrenaline. And in the next chapter, we'll all learn how to manage it for a practice or competitive event — child, adult, coach and competitor.

MIND COACH in Action: Parent's Perspective

" I was getting the sense that neither my teenage son nor my wife wanted me to go to my son's competitions. I can tell you that it was most unsettling and embarrassing, as I realized that I had a few inappropriate behaviors that centered on losing. That's when my son and I decided to take Bob's course together. In just months, my son blossomed in his game. He learned how to deal with his social peer group at school; he learned to be a team leader on his basketball team; and he learned how to improve his grades. But the biggest thing he got was his dad back. Now when I go to competitions, I stay in the Zone and don't even blink when he makes a mistake. No matter when he catches sight of me in the stands, my "MIND COACH" body language reads "the Zone! **"**

— Parent

23 Adrenaline:
Natural Drug of Choice

Ramp yourself up and manage your adrenaline,
all day, every day.

"It is the greatest shot of adrenaline to be doing
what you have wanted to do so badly.
You almost feel like you could fly without the plane."

— **Charles Lindbergh, Star Aviator**

Ten years ago, while working with a number of very competitive, national-level, female figure skaters, I ran up against a wholly unexpected problem: some of them were too demure and quiet. These girls were spending long uninterrupted hours on the ice practicing and the only thing they had to fight was their own self-confidence. As a result, they were like emotional pinballs, knocked hither and thither from emotional crisis to emotional crisis, mental block to mental block, distraction to distraction, coach's tantrum to parent's tantrum. They needed an adrenaline boost to give them some oomph, so I pulled out one of my punching bags and had them kick it. I playfully taunted them to kick harder, and soon they were bowling me over, as figure skaters have very powerful legs meant for jumping…that also work very well for kicking! And once they got a taste of that power, along with the adrenaline that reinforces it, their eyes sparkled and they wanted more of that great feeling.

Contact Sports Generate Continuous Adrenaline — Not

Compare figure skating to football, where athletes have extensive body contact and the pure adrenaline rush of explosive power. Speak to these players and they'll mention their addiction to the adrenaline rush of hitting everything in sight. Add to this their coaches, who get very excited and exuberant and even encourage aggressiveness as a means to raise adrenaline levels. They are quite a different lot, these wired, adrenaline-sated football players. But, sad to say, it is often a crapshoot as to whether or not football players are any more "adrenalized" than figure skaters. The same is true in most sports.

Generally football players know to start the game pumped and ready for action. They scream at each other, hit each other on the pads and have mock one-on-one battles. But, after the game begins, that adrenalized edge is slowly diminished or lost entirely as the adrenaline seeps away. And once that happens, it is very hard to get it back with any degree of certainty.

Pinball Emotions – the Ebb and Flow of the Game

Talk to any athlete or coach and they often speak of *momentum* rather than adrenaline. They speak of tennis matches where one athlete will be down a few sets and slowly the momentum will shift in favor of the other. They speak of golfers who suddenly find the Zone midway in a round and move to an effortless swing. They speak of Olympic-level gymnasts who allow their routines to run effortlessly and mindlessly. We call this momentum but in pure chemical terms it is a stable supply of adrenaline.

These comfortable "adrenalized" states often occur in the middle of competitions when, in my experience, the bags may already be packed for home. If you are not in the Zone and adrenalized at the outset of any match, expect a struggle. It is at best wishful and misguided thinking to expect momentum to build up over the duration of the game. Think of it as a drag race. Both cars build momentum over the course of a quarter mile but the one with the best start and the fastest acceleration wins. Imagine the advantage one of the drivers would have if he hit the start line at full speed. Now, imagine applying that principle to creating adrenaline in your competition.

How much adrenaline do you need to ensure momentum? How much will entrench you in the Zone so that nothing can pull you out? How much is too much, too soon? I was able to answer these questions via karate and I did it in practice sessions by trial and error. First I fled to an isolated region of my house — my basement — when nobody else was home and put on a display more befitting a crazy man. I jumped and screamed and shadow boxed imaginary competitors. I screamed karate yells that even unnerved me — bloodcurdling perhaps.

Initially, I felt a bit wonky (not to mention self-conscious lest the basement's walls be too thin and unable to muffle my yells). I got rubbery legs and glassy, teary eyes. But then I got used to the adrenaline and it felt good — very good. After several sessions of this in the basement, along with testing it in the dojo, I got to the point where I knew precisely how much adrenaline I needed and when. It was a very interesting experiment. The more I pushed myself to higher levels of adrenaline, the easier it was to trigger and control.

Next, on the day of competition, I planned when I would bring on this pre-programmed hyper-adrenaline (not over-adrenaline) state of being. And, it was very exciting, because after I learned to trigger it on demand, I rarely missed the podium. I was that drag racer who was going at full bore at the start line and my opponents never even saw the blur that would pass (beat) them.

Exercise: A-BUTTON (Adrenaline Button)

This exercise can help you to pre-program yourself to "adrenalize" appropriately before any practice or competition. All it takes is pushing the right button — your A-BUTTON.

1) Pick a spot on your body to be your A-BUTTON. (It is an anchor, very much like the anchors you used in Chapter 14.) Choose a spot that is easy for you to touch but is safe from being

accidentally triggered, for, as one of my athletes discovered by accidentally triggering it at bedtime, you may be in for some sleepless nights. Locations on your body that you might use are:

- The fleshy part of the hand between the thumb and the index finger
- The base of the wrist
- The crook of the elbow
- The tip of the nose
- The earlobe

2) Now, remember experiences where you had plenty of adrenaline. A professional surfer I'm working with uses bungee jumping as one of his. Or, you can aggressively shadow box like I did. Or you can remember a sport-related experience. In any case, feel your adrenaline and touch your A-BUTTON.

3) Over the next few days, repeat the exercise several times. You will know when your A-BUTTON is working properly as you will get a surge of adrenaline whenever you touch it. Keep adding new Zone experiences to it to refresh it, especially after competitions where you might have relied on it a lot.

Managing Adrenaline

As far as evoking your adrenaline for competitions, think of it as a simple graph with Amount of Adrenaline (percent) on one axis, and the time (wake up to end of competition) on the other. When you wake up you need to be at X percent adrenaline. When you drive to the venue you need to be at Y percent. When you step onto the ice, court, course or other venue, you need to be at Z percent. With the start of your event, you shift fully to 100 percent fueled and ready to go.   And, of course, your A-BUTTON is always at your fingertips to give you a shot when you need it.

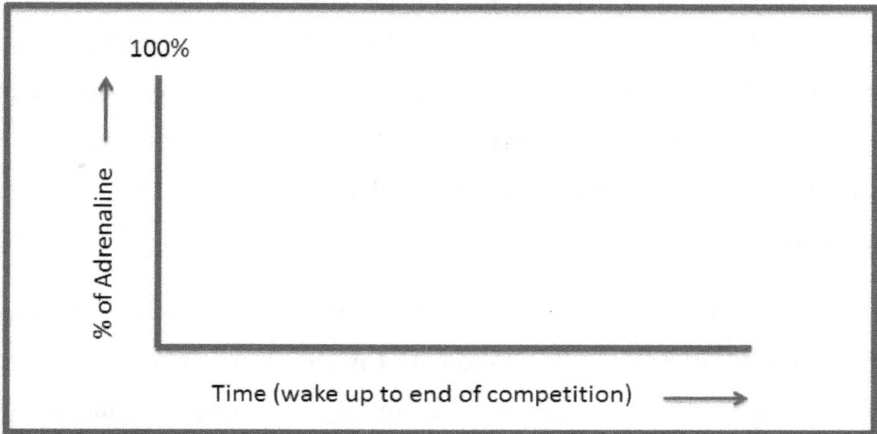

Like any skill, managing your adrenaline level will take some time and practice. With wise management, your body will learn exactly how much you need and when you need it. Eventually you will be able to quickly move into and out of it — at will. But be careful: a young hockey player I worked with made the mistake of firing his adrenaline at the start of the school day and then had none left by the time of his game that evening. Manage your adrenaline output wisely — put it to use when it will be most effective.

Chapter Summary

Just as I've had figure skaters slugging away on punching bags and myself shadowboxing in my basement, all athletes need to create a powerful and accessible supply of adrenaline if they want to win. As well, just as it has to be carefully crafted, it also has to be monitored and adjusted — a process we'll tackle in the next chapter.

A-BUTTON in Action: Sport Leader

❝ During major competitions, as a senior director, I go from event to event to support my coaches and athletes at major competitions. It can be tiring work, even though it might appear like I'm doing very little. For this purpose, I have learned to stay in the Zone, regardless of how individuals on my team are doing and no matter how late in the day it is. And, believe me, standing around keeping your adrenaline high for a full day can be a challenge.

The A-BUTTON helps a lot, as it gives me an additional boost whenever my Zone dips a bit. And until I'm back in my hotel room, I can never lose it. So, when you see me smiling and engaged at the venue, that's my job on game day, with my hand not far from the A-BUTTON. This approach has made a huge difference for my team, and is a lot more fun for me. **❞**

— Sport Leader

24 Never Stop Moving

Adrenaline — Use it or lose it.

"Ninety percent of my game is mental.
It's my concentration that has gotten me this far.
I won't even call a friend on the day of a match.
I'm scared of disrupting my concentration.
I don't allow any competition with tennis."

— Chris Evert, Star Tennis Player

I remember watching the video of a karate tournament in which I had competed. Before the start of the match, the head judge was giving instructions to the black belt combatants, all of whom were standing stock still, except one. He stood out very clearly, a bit silly looking, shifting from foot to foot like a single tree swaying in a perfectly still forest. I looked closely at the person and realized it was ME!

Intuitive Shifting

Now, however, I understand that what I was doing was anything but silly, albeit intuitive. I certainly remember feeling good — and was surely in the Zone — moving to keep my body loose, moving to maintain the adrenaline that I had built up while warming up. I also understand now that my adrenalized swaying was blocking everything else out — my fellow competitors, the judges, the noisy spectators, internal self-talk. Had I stood still, I likely would have felt uncomfortable (as I would have felt my adrenaline seeping away). As for looking silly, that would have been the farthest thing from my mind as that would have required caring about what other people thought of me — which is no way to compete.

In addition to keeping me in the Zone and keeping thoughts out, I soon realized that the swaying had other benefits. When I was training a cross-country ski team for national and international competitions, the coach, a former Olympian, reminded his athletes that awareness of technique in competition is a distraction, as by pushing technique thoughts out of your head, you are trusting that your body and mind will deliver what you need at the time you need it. Nice confirmation.

The shifting stops you from thinking, forcing you to trust the skills you've been practicing — the prerequisite to performing subconsciously. Fueled with sufficient adrenaline and feeling your Zone FEEL, you keep your brain running optimally with no need to think. This is similar to your skills driving a car where, with experience, you can adjust the radio, eat a burger and chat with fellow passengers — with no thoughts of your foot pressure on the gas pedal, grip tension of your hand on the steering wheel or the road vibrations on your backside. Your driving skills work subconsciously. Driving is a FEEL game. Sport needs to be as well — skills, strength, visual acuity, agility and smoothness. The following exercise will help you to develop your 'feel' game and utilize a constant swaying motion to do so. It will keep you trusting your technique, experience and preparedness — without having to think. You will simply run on automatic, fueled by adrenaline.

Exercise: POWER SHIFT

1) Stand upright and imagine that a person is standing beside you, only slightly off your line of center. That person looks like you, YOU in the Zone.

2) Shift from foot to foot, into and through this image, back and forth, repeatedly, like an inverted pendulum. Each time you pass through the image, notice that you can feel your Zone FEEL, which is great GPS.

3) Continue to sway through the image in this manner and allow the adrenaline to super-charge your Zone. It will displace all other thoughts and you'll notice that there is no thinking.

Our competitions allow us ample opportunity to stand still and become sitting ducks for comments, visual distractions and sounds. POWER SHIFT ensures that you keep moving. It was what I was doing at the karate tournament, what many professional athletes do during the singing of the national anthem in preparation for the game, and it is what you'll need to do in the minutes leading up to your competition and between times at bat, on the bench or on the sidelines. It may look odd on camera and it may irritate your opponents, but no one will enter your headspace and you will never be wanting for adrenaline. If you are a competitor who knows your outcome, feels your Zone and trusts in your technique, it'll help you to stay in the Zone all the time — and on the leaderboard.

Chapter Summary

By swaying in POWER SHIFT, you displace thoughts about score, weather, your competition, your work, etc. It keeps the Zone simple and powerful and adrenalized. Watch any professional sports game and you'll see it in action as they shift back and forth — wired to within an inch of their lives and looking totally calm. And what's more, you'll keep your brain incredibly quiet, and, continuing with the computer metaphor, impenetrable to the 'hacking' efforts of others. This facilitates a very efficient way of performing that we'll identify and apply in the next chapter, called QUIET MIND.

POWER SHIFT in Action: Equestrian

❝ An equestrian is part of a team. We are two athletes, not one, and my horse is very sensitive to my state of mind. Nervousness at competitions is clearly a distraction to us both. After I'd learned to stay in the Zone, we began to perform effortlessly, but the pressure-filled seconds before entering the ring were hard to overcome. I tried POWER SHIFT to quiet my internal thoughts, but the swaying drove my equine partner nuts. Bob suggested I be subtle and move a single finger up and down in time to the pace of my (Zone) breathing. That single finger movement allowed me to maintain the pace, which maintained my Zone and kept me thought-free — and our team of two focused. ❞

— Equestrian

25 QUIET MIND — Optimum Brain Power

The means to prevent your brain from rebooting.

"Let's not look back in anger, forward in fear,
but around in awareness."

— **James Thurber, Star Humorist**

As a high performance trainer, I've been working with coaches and athlete across many sports and it has allowed me to see how high-performance strategies are interrelated. One of the most intriguing human facilities is a phenomenon that has been dubbed *Quiet Eye* by Dr. Joan Vickers of Calgary, Canada (Harle, S. & Vickers, J.N., 2001. *Training quiet eye improves accuracy in the basketball free throw.* The Sport Psychologist, 15, 289-305.) Simply, by "quieting" our eyes, we focus better on the task at hand (net opening, strike zone, surrounding players, etc.) and become much more accurate.

Much emphasis in Dr. Vickers' research is directed to the role of the eyes — which is where the term Quiet Eye comes from — and, although the quieting of the eyes are an important part of the equation, they are merely one component of the phenomena that includes your visual, auditory and kinesthetic awareness, your efficient control of adrenaline, oxygen and body temperature and your ability to slow down the pace of the game and readily anticipate what will happen next. All these benefits are indicative of your brain functioning at an optimum level with a very quiet mind. You may continue to refer to the process as Quiet Eye if you like, but when you have had the opportunity to experience it, you'll understand why the eye is only one indicator of a truly exceptional process that I refer to as QUIET MIND (QM).

The Dilemma

The main reason I prefer a broader definition is that focusing on the eye alone can lead us to some misdirection and misunderstanding. In Dr. Vickers' research (where miniature cameras were used to track the eyes) a rather straightforward strategy was used wherein basketball foul-shooters paused for an optimum period of time to prepare the eyes before shooting the shot. The results were phenomenal in the consistency of the resulting shots. However, the dilemma here is that if the process works so well for foul shots, it must work just as well for jump-shots, lay-ups, overhead shots and pivoting shots (and soccer and hockey shots as well). But how would you set up an "optimum" time for those? So I'm going to suggest that more is better; and that you need to be living and playing in QM all the time, not just when you step up to the foul-shot line in basketball, into the blocks in track or between the tees in golf.

Computer Mind

In my discussions with Coach Les Greevy, an Olympic Development coach, he told me that by staying in QM you keep your brain functioning like an efficient computer. And, every time there is a change of visual re-focus (such as focusing on the net, then your teammate, then opponent), you jar your mental computer and interrupt or reboot it. So getting into QM for a foul shot is a moot point, as you should already be fully in it.

To put this in a game context, imagine a player looking to his teammate to receive a pass (1). He catches the ball and looks at the opponent he needs to beat (2). He looks to the basketball net to check if a shot is a possibility (3). He looks to the shot clock (4). He looks at three different teammates to pass it to (5, 6 & 7). He looks at the shot clock again (8). He looks at his opponent again (9). He looks at the basket and shoots (10). Each number in brackets represents the rebooting of his human computer, making this player particularly inefficient and frantic. Oh, and he misses the shot.

The professional player, on the other hand, has learned to stay in QM all the time. He sees the passer, opponent, teammates, clock, basketball and net all at the same time (1) in a peripheral gaze. His brain rarely reboots unless he gets an elbow in the eye. It runs efficiently for the entire game and it knows precisely where everyone is on the court. Oh, and he swishes the shot without thinking.

QM by Any Name has a Long History

In my training in the martial art of karate, I read about QM in ancient Chinese military literature as "looking at the mountain in order to see the person (in front of you)." In Zen literature it appears as "looking in the pond and seeing the mountains." And, in the mid-1970s, in NLP (Neuro-Linguistic Programing) it is referred to it as "Stop The World," because time seems to slow down or stand still. So, it is a very normal phenomenon that has long been understood as being an effective approach to winning in both sport and war.

My professional and Olympic athletes affirm that time does appear to slow down and their reflexes appear faster, and they seem to be able to predict events with uncanny accuracy. They speak of being observers in their own competition where intended targets seem to move slowly and appear huge. They speak of floating over hurdles effortlessly. And they all report that self-talk (both positive and negative) disappears, the brain becomes quiet and their skills run on autopilot.

Exercise: QUIET MIND

Purpose: To achieve your brain's optimum performance

Exercise:

1) To experience QM, look out of a window to a distant object such as a flagpole. Bring your index fingers directly in front of your eyes at arm's length and look through them and remain focused on the flagpole. The fingers will be unfocused.

2) Slowly move your arms outwards to the sides while you continue to stare in the distance. Wiggle your fingers if you need to keep them obvious as you move your arms to the sides. Stop your fingers at the edge of your peripheral vision. You will now see the object in the distance and the wiggling fingers on both sides of your head, all at the same time.

3) Leave your arms extended and notice the sense of observing everything. Notice how quiet your brain becomes. This is QM,

"Quiet Eye," "looking at the mountain in order to see the person (in front of you)," "looking in the pond and seeing the mountains" and "Stop the World." It may feel strange initially, but drop your arms and continue to hold the feeling for as long as you can and experience the wonder of a quiet mind and a self-talk-free mind at that!

4) Now imagine playing your game in QM and notice how your vision is peripheral and you react quickly to game situations.

Additional Exercises

Here are some ways you can build competence with QM so that you learn to live and compete in it all the time:

1) When driving your car, notice how you can see the road ahead and the road behind AT THE SAME TIME (with the help of the rearview mirror, of course). For those of you who are concerned about staying on the road or your braking response time, you had better skip this one. Although, as one might expect, the racecar drivers I work with use QM all the time.

2) Go out on a basketball court (even if you are not a basketball player) and throw some hoops. First do it by constantly refocusing (rebooting the mind) between ball and basketball net. Then do it in QM where you are looking peripherally and the net is only a part of the big picture. Compare the two experiences. Play a pick-up game in QM and notice your awareness of the whole court.

3) Stand on a people-mover, such as at an airport, and allow the world to "stop" around you as you settle into QM and travel through the

spacious building. Notice the quietness of your mind.

4) For those of you who are coaches, practice QM when you are training your students. Stay in it for the whole instructional period and notice how it is different from the times you constantly looked from student to student. It will provide some very interesting perspectives and be a model for your students as well.

5) For those of you who are runners or cyclists who have to contend with hills, you may notice that on the open stretches of your cycle or run that your vision is peripheral and you are looking far into the distance. But, as soon as you approach a hill, your vision changes to a spot on the road just a few feet in front of you and a barrage of self-talk ensues. Force your vision out to both sides of the road, as doing so will get you back into QM and quiet your brain.

6) For those of you who are martial artists or wrestlers, place your gaze well beyond your opponent as though you are "looking at a mountain." Your opponent will still be in full view and your peripheral vision will be taking in everything, no matter what is thrown at you.

Chapter Summary

QUIET MIND can feel quite strange at the outset, so practice these activities until QM feels normal off your court, ice, field, etc. Once you're comfortable staying in it, go test it out in your practices. Notice how quiet your brain is and how focused you are. And, when you get really comfortable in practice, it should begin to happen automatically in your game. Quite simply, when QM 'stops' the noisiness in your head, you are optimizing your brain.

QUIET MIND is the last of the tools in Step 4 of the SportExcel System. Now, just like you need to trust that your sport skills will work for you without thinking, you also need to trust that the skills you are learning in this book are working for you — without having to think about them either. Our subconscious mind really is very capable of doing this — with little or no conscious thinking. In the next section, Step 5 of the SportExcel System, we'll find out how.

QUIET MIND in Action: Collegiate Hockey

❝ I wouldn't wish a concussion on my worst enemy. It was the reason I went to Bob as I was still struggling with post-concussion symptoms. Using the various tools, I learned to resolve the symptoms of the concussion and to forget the original memory of my head hitting the boards. What was even more amazing, developing QUIET MIND enabled me to see the whole ice surface, which is a pretty neat ability when it comes to helping a hockey player like me avoid collisions, intentional or otherwise. Missing one year of hockey is enough! **❞**

— Hockey Player

STOP

Put one tool at the top of each day on your calendar and practice it each day until you understand and can use it effortlessly.

Step 5

The System

The beauty of setting up a system is that it will work for you and make your life a lot easier, even when you are sleeping.

"Success isn't something that just happens — success is learned, success is practiced and then it is shared."

— Sparky Anderson, Star Baseball Coach

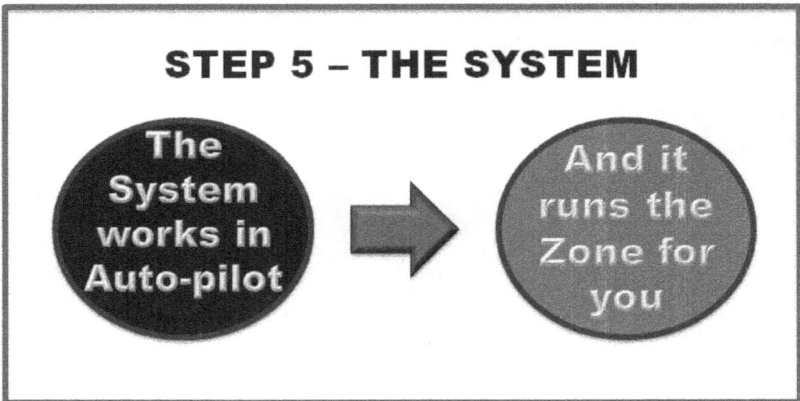

STEP 5 – THE SYSTEM

The System works in Auto-pilot ➡ And it runs the Zone for you

26 Building Trust: On Autopilot

Keep the Zone running 24/7.

"Before I'd get in the ring, I'd have already won or lost it on the road. The real part is won or lost somewhere far away from witnesses — behind the lines, in the gym and out there on the road, long before I dance under those lights."

— *Muhammad Ali, Star "Float like a butterfly, sting like a bee" Boxer*

Just as many of you anticipate the start of your season, I look forward to a summer of recreational golf. Ah, warm summer days, great enduring friendships, singing birds, gem-green landscapes. In this idyllic setting, one can almost hear gentle symphonic music in the background. Why, it is so beautiful it begs the old expression, "A bad day on the golf course is better than a good day in the office."

If you knew my dark sense of humor, you would be waiting for someone to jar the CD player to start the beautiful music st-st-st-stuttering.

Golf, or any other sport, whether recreational or competitive, is rarely like that. In the brief moments when you are hearing yourself say that you love the sport, there is another person who insists on thwacking the CD player. In very pleasant, under-the-radar tones during normal conversation, he or she will say: "Hey, you're swinging well, what are you doing different?" Or, "That new club seems to be working great." Or, "Hitting the greens sure is tough with that wind." Or, "That club's not working for you, is it?"

As I've previously stated in this book, to be in the Zone you must be playing without thinking, in a kind of trance at the subconscious level. The probable intent of a partner's statements is to break the trance and bring you back to the conscious realm. The partner might as well be saying, "Hey, you're not thinking of anything but golf (you're beating us) and we need to get you to think about something else (so you'll lose)."

Subconscious Competence

A skillful Zone is often referred to as Subconscious Competence — you don't have to think about what you're doing anymore; you're just good at it subconsciously — and it requires incredible TRUST in your abilities. When you are in this state, the game is easy. There is no self-talk and especially no easy explanation of what is happening; it just happens without thinking. (Sometimes we are even watching ourselves perform.) We need to learn how to engage our subconscious mind in this process, every time.

I learned about subconscious competence through karate. At the time, I was good at sparring but reluctant to compete because I second-guessed myself and listened to all manner of self-talk. "Jim has long legs, so go in tight; Bill is fast, so give him some distance; Richard is tricky, so watch his fakes." I became more concerned about what they could do to me rather than what I had to do to them, and I forgot to fight. I had no trust in my ability to protect myself — I was scared.

In hockey it was different. I not only trusted that my legs would skate for me without thinking, I never even thought about them. Every part of me and every piece of equipment was non-existent; I just *was*. My skates were my feet, my gloves and stick were my hands and my pads were my skin. When I played, I knew they would work for me. I never even thought that I carried around 30 pounds of equipment until it was all in one bag and I had to lug it to the car.

My Experiment

I knew that somehow I had to get to that same level of subconscious competence in karate. Somehow I had to trust that my arms and feet would take care of me, that they would automatically do what I had spent years training them to do — block kicks and punches and deliver offensive power — without having to think about it at all.

I can honestly tell you that I initially had no idea how to get to this skill level. But an idea occurred to me — another experiment. Where I got the idea I'll never know but it was one of those ideas that seemed good at the time. So, in my next practice, I made a conscious decision to stop blocking all attacks, both kicks and punches. Now, this experiment was performed in the relative safety of a karate practice, although none of my opponents were let in on what I was doing — nor, I presume, would they have cared.

My experiment was not without risk. Although no contact to the head was allowed, we usually permitted "some" body contact during sparring. The higher the belt level, the more contact you got and were expected to take. So, as the first match commenced, I took one hard hit after another. I sidestepped to avoid attacks and remained resolutely block-less. I made every effort to "not think" about blocking, no matter what. In this case, it hurt a great deal to "not think".

It Worked

After several fights, my fellow karate practitioners showed no signs of acknowledging my blocking incompetence, nor did they show sympathy. They had me in pain — my ribs hurt, by chest had welts caused by knuckles twisting my gi (tunic or uniform) — and I imagined that they were enjoying it! But underlying my pain I felt a strange sensation. It grew stronger from sparring match to sparring match, stronger and stronger, until — I'm not sure when or in what fight it happened — I exploded with a bewildering barrage of punches and kicks at one of my opponents. *Wow,* I remember saying to myself, *this is cool.* And I did it without thinking.

My explanation is this: in the midst of this painful experiment, my subconscious mind must have gotten frustrated and angry, and then rebelled, as if to say, "If you are not going to block, I will!" Whatever the explanation, it was the turning point in my career and I never had to think about blocking again — my subconscious mind did it for me from that point on. I had only to set the offensive outcome of winning and my arms and legs and body knew exactly what to do and when. It was the kind of TRUST I would bring to every future competition.

Exercises: TRUST BUILDING

In all sports, you must TRUST in your abilities and strategies, including those you have learned in this book. There can be no thought or self-talk. Your equipment must simply be an extension of your arms. You must learn to let your subconscious mind perform. Making mistakes and correcting for them via correction routines or correction reflexes via GPS will perfect the process. The following are exercises that will help you to learn to trust your skills. Some may not be applicable to your sport so you may have to adapt them. Like me, experiment with these kinds of exercises to move your game to the level of TRUST.

1) Get yourself so exhausted you can hardly stand up. Do this by physical activity — a long workout, plus a five-mile run, plus 100 pushups. Then, without resting, focus purely on getting your Zone and apply your A-BUTTON. Your conscious mind will be so focused on overcoming your exhaustion — your labored breathing, heavy arms and shaky legs — that thinking will be impossible. (Only do this if you are fit and healthy and with a doctor's approval.)

2) For sports where you need to do routine movements such as a golf swing without thinking, you can mentally visualize some other activity such as a swimmer's breaststroke. You get in the Zone and occupy your conscious mind by envisioning the repetitive breaststroke, and then proceed with your routine. For example, I encourage my karate students to maintain the breaststroke throughout their kata-forms routine. If they get lost at some point in the routine, they apply a strategy such as

TALENT MODE or FUSING at that spot to resolve whatever stopped them, and then do it again. It can be highly effective for testing out routines that should be running subconsciously. Oh, and when you do it, enjoy the swim.

3) Set your eyes and brain in QUIET MIND and play your game.

4) Wear an iPod and listen to music. With some attention to volume level so as not to damage your hearing, get in the Zone by concentrating on the emotion of the music. With your conscious mind nicely distracted, your subconscious mind will be free to perform for you.

5) Adapt my karate "trust" exercise to your sport. With this exercise, get yourself completely wired to perform (with lots of adrenaline), and force yourself to hold back until your subconscious rebels and triggers your play with no thinking. See if you can feel your subconscious mind engage and initiate your sport routine, whatever it is. In basketball, for example, you could have someone feed you balls repeatedly and very quickly, so that you have to shoot without any set up and from all positions, especially awkward ones. And in golf, for example, you can play what is called, 'speed golf.' You still follow your routines but speed them up. In this case, make sure you follow all course rules, perhaps even getting your coach's or parent's approval if you are a minor.

The objective of these exercises is to distract the conscious mind from the task and to let your subconscious mind do what it is good at. You want to be running on automatic which creates a fantastic Zone feeling with no thought. Your equipment is a part of you and could just as easily be an extension of your arm. All routines are automatic. The swish of the basket — was that you who just pumped that shot?

Chapter Summary

By TRUSTING in your abilities, you can develop your skills so that nothing, not even distracting comments from your peers, can affect you or your Zone. In the next chapter we'll take this concept and all the other tools you have learned and create an unflappable attitude, so that making a mistake or completely falling apart becomes part of the learning experience — something to laugh at and get excited about.

27 Now That's Attitude

Learning to apply the system in a dynamic way.

"When someone tells me there is only one way to do things, it always lights a fire under my butt. My instant reaction is, I'm gonna prove you wrong."

— ***Picabo Street, Star Skier***

I work with many different sports and many great passionate athletes, and I get a few that require attitude adjustments. They simply lack something. This kind of athlete makes any number of excuses for not winning (and sometimes even for winning). They relate failure to coaches, parents, equipment and even the weather. A few rightfully place the blame squarely on their own shoulders but even this can be counterproductive. Blaming, making excuses and targeting oneself are only helpful from the perspective of your opponents (i.e., they don't have to do it to you if you're doing it to yourself).

Passion Trumps Skill

I'll take passionate athletes with developing skills any day over those who are disinterested yet have fabulous skills. I've been working with just such an athlete for several years — a young hockey player — the one who just signed a pro contract. He has passion, tenacity and a never-say-die attitude. Initially he had limited confidence, but quickly and surely he developed into a skillful, dynamic and confident athlete.

He also had many disappointments, such as the time he failed to make a provincial team. Afterwards, his dad told me that camp had gone well and he'd never seen his son play better. It had been a tremendous experience for him, and yet he suspected his son might be greatly disappointed. Hence, when he asked me to speak to him, I was expecting the worst.

In our next clinic, the young man was anything but dejected. He spoke excitedly of the training camp, the mental training he had gotten, the high intensity scrimmages and the opportunity to raise his game to another level by playing with many other talented athletes. He had a fire in his eyes and I was a bit shocked by his exuberance. I asked him what he wanted to do next. "I want to get better," he said. "I now know I need to be a smarter player." I smiled. Here he was giving me the pep talk. Now that's ATTITUDE!

View of the World

Attitude — how you view the world — is critically important as it affects your resiliency. You immediately forget mistakes and move on, or you carry them for the rest of the competition, perhaps all your life. There are so many things that can negatively affect your game. Friends or parents may be watching. An overly hot venue may cause dehydration and fatigue. An adjustment to your equipment is awkward and bothersome. An old sports injury acts up. And with all or some of the above, you could still show great ATTITUDE by sticking to your game.

On another day, everything goes well. There was something special in the coffee. Your teammates are all in the Zone. Camaraderie is fantastic. Scoring comes easily. You get lots of slaps on the back as you play without thinking. And you show great ATTITUDE by walking around tall and encouraging others.

We are initially oblivious to our ATTITUDE. We bounce back when we're young, just as we bounced back from repeated falling when we learned to walk. Then, after a certain age, we start to become self-conscious of how we perform. We search for reasons for awful performances, such as blaming others, blaming ourselves, creating excuses. If we are used to being great because of inferior opponents or because of our ability, when the game gets a little more competitive our self-worth may get tainted by failure. We get embarrassed, defensive and impatient with ourselves and others. Our self-worth gets tied to our score, and we can begin to show some serious ATTITUDE defects, such as throwing tantrums. No one wants us around.

System Dynamics: Outcome, GPS and Tools

In order to prevent ATTITUDE from degenerating into anti-social behaviors, we need to take advantage of every experience — losses, mistakes and even wins. We need to know our OUTCOME, and that we will eventually get what we want, as perceived in our DÉJÀ-VU DVD. We need to understand that everything is GPS — and nothing is bad, negative, stupid or makes us an inferior human being. And we need to always act on GPS with TOOLS — FUSING, TALENT MODE, VISTA, and so on, and never quit.

Every experience gives you GPS and reveals information that, once processed, can propel you toward your OUTCOME. In the absence of blaming, beating yourself up, gloating etc., you have an incredible opportunity to learn. By stopping the negative from creeping in, you start to perceive the obvious and the subtle — and everything in between.

The young hockey player is an example of this. After every game he asks, "How can I get better and smarter?" With every injury he asks, "How can I get stronger and stay injury free?" And with very person who pulls him out of the Zone, he asks, "What can I do to prevent that or intimidate him instead?" The diagram illustrates how this kind of thinking keeps looping back in a way that moves us closer and closer to our outcome — when we are persistent.

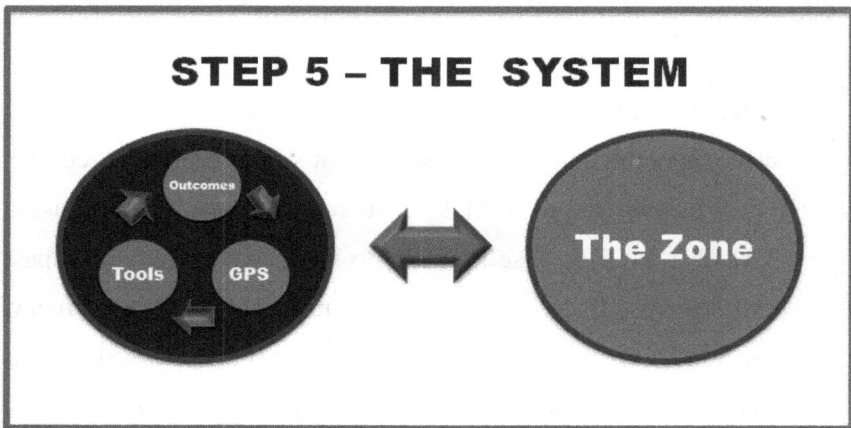

STEP 5 – THE SYSTEM

Outcomes

Tools   GPS

The Zone

This is a simple process that, when displayed to those around us, comes across as great attitude. There is never frustration or doubt about the outcome. Getting cut in hockey or missing putts in golf is simply GPS. The athlete acts on the GPS by using technical or mental strategies and then tests out the changes. Each change gets him or her closer to the outcome and the loop begins again. That, in essence, is a great, never-say-die ATTITUDE.

Exercise: ATTITUDE in Action

Since everyone can see ATTITUDE in other people's postures, let's use this measure in an attitude-building exercise for ourselves:

1) Remember a less-than-stellar performance in your game. Step back and examine your image closely using MIND COACH. Notice the tension or the hang-dog look or the redness in your face due to frustration. Then take another mental image, this time of an elite athlete, pro or Olympian, and put him or her on the same field beside you and compare his or her image to your own. What do you notice? What are the differences? (Size or brightness, etc.)

2) Once you have a clear idea of the differences, make some changes to the image of yourself. That's right. Simply "redraw" your mental image. Make yourself look skillful by using TALENT MODE. Use FUSING to bring in some powerful past experiences. If the image appears too dark or distant or fuzzy, use VISTA to make it crystal clear and bright and focused. If you think it still looks a bit lame, press your A-BUTTON. And finally, check for QUIET MIND.

3) Once you are satisfied with the similarity of your image to the model you picked, step onto the stage into the shoes of the new you and then go test it out.

4) At various stages in your year, reassess this image and continue to evolve into the athlete you wish to become.

When you do this exercise you are acting on various forms of GPS, both the good and the bad. It is up to you to stay in the posture of that model through thick and thin. After every competition, you can re-evaluate how you did and loop back through the process. Like any strategy, it takes practice; it takes persistence; and it takes attitude. Rather, it *IS* ATTITUDE.

Chapter Summary

Various attitudes such as blaming, using excuses, beating ourselves up or bragging (with a loss or a win) cloud our ability to challenge ourselves to become skillful athletes and keen competitors. We need to KNOW our Outcomes, ACT on the GPS and continually APPLY proper TOOLS. When we KNOW, ACT and APPLY the SportExcel System fluidly, we will have the kind of ATTITUDE that will ensure we start to win consistently. And, in the next chapter, I'll explain how dealing with the trauma of failure not only builds great ATTITUDE, but it is also the only way we can gain perspective and grow.

28 Attitude in Action

Post-Traumatic Growth; what doesn't kill you

makes you stronger.

"You miss 100 percent of the shots you never take."

— *Wayne Gretzky, Star Hockey Player*

Before coming to see me, a number of my clients have been so discouraged that they asked themselves why they bothered to compete, why they put themselves on the line in front of their peers, why they accepted humiliation and then came back for more.

This human, competitive nature of needing to compete and needing to compare your ability to another's is very intriguing. It is helpful to have a great ATTITUDE from the outset in order to get through the trauma that can result from our need to compete and compare. Having great attitude shows you can process information subconsciously in a critical manner, with maturity and wisdom — the "glass half full" kind of competitor.

Athlete versus Comic

Being a competitive athlete is very similar to being a stand-up comic. The disciplines have four things in common:

- When each one makes mistakes, the result is immediately evident.
- They each have hecklers (sometimes merely imagined but not always).
- They each require good timing (skill).
- And, importantly, the only way to learn how to perform is to get up there and fail — the more times the better.

Although I have described how DÉJÀ-VU DVD is a great aid in preparing for competitions, the only way to get realistic guidance from your mistakes is to learn "on the job." Initially, comics tell jokes poorly or misread the audience and get heckled. Initially, athletes have poor skills or misread the game and accept "friendly" barbs. Both put their honor, pride, self-esteem and man/womanhood on the line each time. And yet there is no other sensation quite like it, no other way to do it, and we all love it when we're on and even sometimes when we're not.

"What is a grown man like me doing standing up here in front of my peers making a fool of myself?" is the question one athlete asked after his first few disastrous experiences. Coupled with his negative self-talk were a churning stomach, gurgling bowels, and a body soaked with sweat externally and adrenaline internally. He was quite delighted to hear that there is a term for his trial by fire — Post-traumatic Growth, the flip side to the Post-traumatic Stress Disorder we hear so much about in the news, especially with regard to returning servicemen and women. In sports, Post Traumatic Growth (PTG) justifies our putting ourselves in "harm's way" with the expectation (vision) that we will eventually get that perfect score.

Post-traumatic Growth

"Post-traumatic growth is a process people go through in the aftermath of experiencing trauma," said Dr. Robert Tedeschi, Professor of Psychology at the University of North Carolina at Charlotte when he addressed the Command and General Staff, college students and staff at Fort Leavenworth, Kansas. "It's also an outcome of trauma. It's a series of changes people experience themselves that they label as valuable, or beneficial, maybe not right away, but in the long run. Traumatic experience can be transformative in some people, putting them on a whole new life path."

What this suggests is that people have the ability to learn from their experiences, no matter how traumatic. The words of Friedrich Neitzsche, "What doesn't kill you makes you stronger," come to mind. The challenge with concepts like PTG is to teach ourselves the specifics of how to turn trauma into opportunities for growth.

Losing in sports can be traumatic; taking the flak from your friends on your team can be traumatic; the embarrassment of telling your spouse how poorly you did can be traumatic; wasting away at a plateau while your colleagues have moved on can be traumatic. Perhaps these traumas are not on the scale of the human trauma that Dr. Tedeschi is talking about, but it is the same process, and the tools you have learned in this book will help you to grow beyond it.

A New Way of Thinking

You have learned tools that will help you to shrink any problem. You have learned a new way of thinking, one that allows you to evaluate your performance, no matter how bad the pain is. You have learned to set your own path to what you want with DÉJÀ-VU DVD. You have learned to see the world from the viewpoint of elite athletes through TALENT MODE. You have learned to step back and be the spectator of how others affect you via MIND COACH. And, with all the other tools you have learned — FUSING, POWER WALK, POWER SHIFT, VISTA, A-BUTTON and QUIET MIND — you know how to make adjustments and move on. No longer do you have to despair over the prospect of performing poorly.

Lose or win, you can take all the tools the SportExcel System has to offer and incorporate these tools into your game at the subconscious level so that you grow in your ability to perform before, during and after your competition. The more you put yourself on the line, the more you grow — Post Traumatic Growth.

Chapter Summary

So, whether you are getting people to laugh as a stand-up comic, or getting them to stop laughing as an athlete, you are pushing yourself to overcome trauma and exercising your potential for growth. To quote Dr. Tedeschi again, "It's not the trauma that changes people, it's the struggle." The SportExcel System will help you with your own personal and performance struggles in sport, in life and in your relationships. In the last chapter, I'll put the responsibility to grow squarely in your court, because the tools I've been teaching you don't do the work, you do. And you now have the means to transform your game.

Make sure you practice fixing the blocks in your game until a winning attitude becomes subconscious and automatic.

Reference: Dr. Robert Tedeschi, Professor of Psychology at the University of North Carolina, Charlotte to the Command and General Staff, college students and staff about *"Posttraumatic Growth and Combat: Seeing possibilities for growth and ways of promoting it"* in the Lewis and Clark Center's Eisenhower Auditorium, Fort Leavenworth, Kansas.

http://www.army.mil/-news/2010/04/09/37139-expert-discusses-benefits-of-post-traumatic-growth

Step 6

All About YOU

The System Works (When You Do)

"You are never really playing an opponent. You are playing yourself, your own highest standards, and, when you reach your limits, that is real joy."

— Arthur Ash, Star Tennis Player

STEP 6 – YOU

It is up to YOU to do it ➡ And make the Zone a way of being

29 It is all about YOU (Applying the System)

Enjoy the Zone and go play — in practice and in competition.

"I always practice as I intend to play."

— Jack Nicklaus, Star Golfer

This, the final chapter, is when most books draw conclusions and draw to an end. But for you it is the beginning, the start of new perceptions, strategies, outlooks and outcomes. This is where we establish a commitment to excellence, where, to paraphrase Vince Lombardi, we strive for perfection and settle for excellence.

You now have a beginning, a system unlike any other for winning by getting in the Zone and maintaining it. The tools of the system are very powerful, and — based on my findings and results with hundreds of athletes and many thousands of hours of training — easy to learn and apply. My athletes win; my coaches win. The insights and practical applications of the SportExcel System resulted in many positive changes in teams, coaches and athletes — personal bests, great relationships, rewarding experiences, business leadership skills, educational enhancement, balanced lives and other bonuses of competing to win.

The New Way — A Repeatable System

And now, you too possess what each of my athletes, coaches and sport leaders has, a new way of looking at your sport — with a repeatable system in six steps. Like them, you have Step 1 of the SportExcel System, the Zone, and the means to get into it via Zone FEEL and NO-Zone FEEL, both absolutely critical signals. And you now have every opportunity to live in the Zone, all the time, no excuses.

You now know the importance of Step 2 of the SportExcel System, of having your OUTCOME bright and bold and adrenalized — DÉJÀ-VU DVD. Outcomes made real.

You now know the importance of Step 3 of the SportExcel System, of utilizing the good, the bad and the ugly as GPS or guidance. What doesn't kill you makes you stronger.

You now know the importance of Step 4 of the SportExcel System, and the tools that can flip you back into the Zone in the blink of the eye. You have FUSING to help you forget, TALENT MODE to help you to learn, VISTA to help make intended targets bigger, MIND COACH to help deal with difficult people, POWER WALK and POWER SHIFT to help develop and maintain your Zone. You have the A-BUTTON to control your adrenaline. And you have QUIET MIND for optimum performance with no self-talk. It is quite the tool kit. Use it.

You now know the importance of putting it all together at the subconscious level with Step 5 of the SportExcel System, where you loop through the system and get stronger and more skillful.   Ultimately, through setting proper outcomes, testing them out in practice and competition and breaking through blocks and frustration time and again, you'll understand that losing your Zone FEEL is simply GPS — the symptom — and you now have the means — the tools — to move on.

All Sports, All Disciplines

The SportExcel System works with all sports: soccer, golf, baseball, hockey, badminton, tennis, football, snowboarding, surfing, etc. It also works with business, the arts, healthcare, education and any other discipline you can think of. It is purely educational, not an attempt to fix you with psychology. It is strategy-based, just as mathematics is number and equation-based. You will not be "fixed" by this high performance approach, but you will now have a solid foundation of strategies with which to train yourself and to be competitive at any level, any age.

It Doesn't Work — You Do

So, take your new tools and apply them — to every part of your game. Be skeptical if you must, but give the system a chance. This is Step 6 of the SportExcel System. The system doesn't work, you do. The tools don't work, you do. And, in order for you to work, you need to practice.

Create a calendar for your training schedule and put a different tool at the top of each day — DÉJÀ-VU DVD on Monday, FUSING on

Tuesday, TALENT MODE on Wednesday, etc. On that day, practice that tool over and over until it becomes easy to use. On the next day, practice the next tool, and so on. Every time you apply a tool, it will become easier to use and ultimately will become so ingrained in your subconscious that it will be applied instantly in a crisis, just as quickly as the answer of "2 + 2" comes to mind.

Here are a few parting shots:

- As you are now fully on the road to excellence, you may want to go on this journey with someone: your coach. No matter how good your mental game is, or how mature you are, or how successful you are in other sports or business, everyone needs a coach. The cost will be worth it.

- Stay healthy on this journey — eat healthy, drink in moderation, cross train, get therapeutic help with injuries, etc. You know the routine. If for no other reason, do it to maintain your strength and flexibility, especially as you grow older. Besides, it just feels good being healthy.

- The Zone is a skill, and just like any other skill, it needs to be practiced.

- Enjoy the Zone and go have some fun with practice and play — and win. Winning is not the only reason you will want to continue with your sport, as more often than not enjoyment is a pretty high requirement. But winning was an essential ingredient for me and I suspect for you as well. Go for it.

- Call me if you want more guidance (one-on-one training, training tune-ups, parent/young athlete training or in-person clinics) as I'm very good at GPS when you have overlooked something.

- And lastly, if anyone tells you to set realistic goals because only one percent of athletes will ever be pros or Olympians, I say, YOU strive to be the one percent.

My wish for you is great play, great enjoyment, and great growth, whatever your sport and whatever your projected level of attainment.

Meet the Author

Bob Palmer, B.Ed., B.E.S.
CEO, High Performance Strategist and Trainer, SportExcel Inc.

Bob Palmer founded SportExcel Inc. in 1994, driving 21st century high-performance innovation that is transforming how athletes, coaches and sports organizations achieve their dreams. A respected and inspiring industry leader and expert, Palmer has been instrumental in pioneering a non-psychology approach that is revolutionizing the sports industry.

The SportExcel system has been embraced by a wide range of sports including the clay target sports, surfing, snowboarding, skateboarding, triathlon and golf as well as the team sports of football, hockey, baseball and soccer. It has ignited the passion, joy and skillfulness of athletes and coaches. Athletes in a number of sports, including the shooting sports, have achieved podium success in the Olympics, Pan Am Games, X Games and Commonwealth Games as a result.

A professional educator, Palmer holds a degree in Education from Brock University, a degree in Environmental Studies from the University of Waterloo and a Master Practitioner level in neuro-linguistic training. He writes on high performance and leadership for Trap & Field Magazine, Skeet Shooting Review and several on-line magazines and newsletters. A 4th degree black belt, Palmer is the High Performance Trainer for the Shintani Wado Kai Karate National Team.

Training Resources

SportExcel athletes and coaches live all over the world and the SportExcel system is tailored to transcend geography. We offer a variety of training options to move your sport to the next level – from free introductory sessions and seven week training programs via Skype with Bob Palmer to high performance clinics at your location. We also have a free resource library of articles, videos and podcasts on our website, on our blog and on YouTube.

Whether you live in the U.S., Canada, Australia, Europe, Asia or anywhere else, we are just a phone call, Skype call or email away to getting you in the Zone.

High Performance Clinics

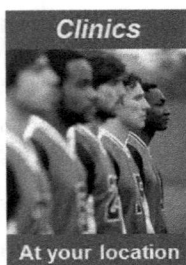

Clinics

At your location

SportExcel delivers engaging one-day high performance clinics throughout North America and beyond. We will travel to your location and teach your coaches, athletes, team or organization the tools to become the expert in managing their Zone through our cutting-edge, high performance system.

Learn to build incredible focus, model Olympians and pros, develop leadership skills and learn to fix virtually any block to performance. It is a hands-on clinic designed to build camaraderie and teamwork. (Parents often observe or join in.)

One-on-One Skype Training Options

Free Introductory Session

Via Skype, Bob Palmer will give you a hands-on, strategy-based session to introduce you to the SportExcel system, with no financial obligation. You then have the option of continuing your training with our *Ignition* Training Series. Experience SportExcel's innovative, approach to taking your game to the next level.

Ignition Training Series

Acquire a revolutionary approach to winning that helps you to identify your moments of brilliance as your Zone, and gives you powerful tools to support it. Your Zone is the essential part of your sport foundation that you will continually reinforce and refine over the course of this program, your season and your career. This is not psychology. There is no personal sharing or divulging of confidential information required. And parents and young athletes can learn together.

Momentum Training Series

The *Momentum* Series moves powerfully into the leadership realm. It reinforces and builds on the Zone concepts learned in the *Ignition* series training. The training supports athletes, coaches and sport/business leaders who want to achieve the next level in their sport and/or business, by learning the tools for setting powerful outcomes, building persuasive leadership, influencing change and building a strategic personal and leadership framework.

Velocity Training Series

The *Velocity* Series is designed as a mastery program for athletes and coaches who have taken previous SportExcel training and who are now wired to win and simply need fine-tuning to stay on track. It is ideal for yearly maintenance, support for competitions, problem resolution and yearly planning.

Articles, Videos, Blogs, Newsletters and Podcasts

SportExcel has a free resource library of high performance articles, podcasts and videos from high performance trainer, Bob Palmer. They cover a wide range of topics on high performance and can be accessed free of charge at: **www.sportexcel.ca**.

Newsletter

Sign up for our e-newsletter which features high performance training articles, athlete and coach spotlights and other news from the world of high performance. We respect your privacy and will never share your information with others. Go to our website home page and click on the newsletter sign-up box: **www.sportexcel.ca**

Questions? Success Stories?
Contact Us

SportExcel's mission is to transform, empower and inspire athletes and coaches to realize their dreams. Our athletes and coaches live all over the world and the SportExcel system is tailored to transcend geography. We take great pride in our athletes' successes — both local and world class — as well as their heart and determination.

If you have a success story to share with us, a question on what you have read in our book or about our other training resources, please contact us. We would be happy to take a moment to answer your questions, hear about your successes and do what we can to set your sport on the road to winning, leadership and fun.

Call Toll-free in North America: 1.877.967.5747

Call International: 1.705.720.2291

Skype: sportexcel

Email: bpalmer@sportexcel.ca

www.ingramcontent.com/pod-product-compliance
Lightning Source LLC
Chambersburg PA
CBHW071949090426
42740CB00011B/1863